Amish Christmas Cookbook

Amish Christmas Cookbook

AUTHENTIC FAVORITES FROM THREE GENERATIONS OF AMISH COOKS

Linda Byler, Laura Anne Lapp & Anna Kauffman

Good Books

New York, New York

Contents

"And the angel said unto them, Fear not: for, behold, I bring you good tidings of great joy, which shall be to all people. For unto you is born this day in the city of David a Saviour, which is Christ the Lord." —LUKE 2:9-10

A Word About Amish Christmas Traditions

Food wraps through, in, and around Amish social occasions—from Sunday church lunches to neighborhood work parties. Food secures these families. It builds bonds in the Amish faith community. It adds pure pleasure to the lives of these disciplined people. But the Christmas season is a time when delicious food is even more abundant. In December, nearly every Amish kitchen is filled with the sweet aromas of baked goods—cookies, candies, pies, and cakes. And everyone looks forward to *S' Grishtag Essa* (Christmas dinner).

Christmas dinner is one of the most well-established holiday traditions in Amish comminities. Most families are large, so a gathering of fifty to eighty or more is not unusual. Menus will vary for each family, but a dish served often is *Roascht* (page 49), the chicken and bread filling served at our weddings. We also often have ham or turkey, mashed potatoes and chicken gravy, and a wide variety of other sides. Desserts vary from one family favorite to another, but our family favorites are pecan pie (page 127) and date pudding (page 168).

After gifts are exchanged and a healthy round of Christmas hymns sung, we play games of Rook, Monopoly, Settlers, Uno, or Phase 10. The children run wild with their cousins outside in the cold, coming in to replenish their stash of pocketed Christmas candy. Sleepy grandparents recline on comfortable sofas, a smile on their faces, quietly reveling in *die noch kommen schafft* (the coming generation). Treats, snacks, and coffee are always in plentiful supply.

Throughout this book, you'll find more interesting tidbits about Amish traditions. But of course the recipes are the real focus here. Many of these recipes are enjoyed year-round—not just on Christmas Day. We hope you'll enjoy experiencing our food as much as we do!

—Linda Byler and Laura Lapp

Breads and Spreads

Becky Zook Bread

Makes: 5 loaves
Prep Time: 30 minutes
Rising Time: 2–4 hours
Baking Time: 30–40 minutes

4 cups warm (110–112°F) water, *divided*
½ tablespoon dry active yeast
½ cup and ½ tablespoon sugar, *divided*
¼ cup lard or Crisco, melted
1 tablespoon salt
3 quarts Occident* flour

Occident flour is bread flour made from western wheat.

TIP:
To check if the bread is finished, tap the top. Bread is ready when you hear a dull sound.

1. In a small bowl, combine 1 cup water, yeast, and ½ tablespoon sugar. Stir and let stand until bubbly, approximately 2–5 minutes.

2. In another large bowl, mix 3 cups water, ½ cup sugar, lard, and salt.

3. Pour yeast mixture into the large bowl and stir.

4. Using a spoon, beat in flour until too thick to stir. Then, use hands to mix in remaining flour.

5. Knead bread dough until smooth and elastic.

6. Cover with a towel or plastic wrap and set in a warm place to rise. Let rise for 1 hour, or until dough doubles in size.

7. Using fists, punch dough down and remove from bowl.

8. Shape dough into 5 loaves.

9. Place loaves into well-greased loaf pans and let rise for 1 hour, covered, or until dough doubles in size.

10. Bake at 350°F for 30–40 minutes.

Refrigerator Bread

Makes: 2 loaves
Prep Time: 30 minutes
Rising Time: 2–4 hours
Baking Time: 30 minutes

2 packages or 2 tablespoons, dry active yeast
2 cups warm (110–112°F) water
½ cup sugar
⅓ cup vegetable oil
1 egg, beaten
6½–7 cups flour
1 teaspoon salt

1. In a large bowl, dissolve yeast in warm water. Let stand until foamy, approximately 2–5 minutes.

2. Stir in sugar and oil.

3. Add egg, flour, and salt. Knead dough until smooth and elastic.

4. Place dough in a greased bowl. Cover and let rise for 1–2 hours, or until double in size.

5. With fists, punch down dough.

6. Place dough in well-greased loaf pans.

7. Cover. Let rise for 1–2 hours, or until nearly doubled in size.

8. Bake at 350°F for 30 minutes.

VARIATION:

After punching down dough, place covered bowl of dough in refrigerator. Take out fresh bread dough as needed to make bread or rolls. When using dough from refrigerator, allow at least 2–3 hours for dough to warm up and rise before baking.

Oatmeal Bread

Makes: 3 loaves
Prep Time: 30 minutes
Rising Time: 2–4 hours
Baking Time: 30 minutes

2 cups boiling water
1 cup dry quick oats
½ cup whole wheat flour
½ cup brown sugar
1 tablespoon salt
2 tablespoons (¼ stick) butter, softened
1 tablespoon dry active yeast
½ cup very warm (110–115°F) water
5 cups all-purpose flour
Melted butter

1. In a large bowl, pour 2 cups boiling water over dry oatmeal.

2. Stir in whole wheat flour, sugar, salt, and butter.

3. Allow to cool.

4. In a separate bowl, dissolve yeast in ½ cup very warm water.

5. Add yeast to oatmeal mixture.

6. Add all-purpose flour and beat until creamy.

7. Knead dough until smooth and elastic.

8. Cover dough with a towel or plastic wrap, and let rise for 1 hour.

9. With fists, punch down dough.

10. Shape into 3 loaves and put into well-greased loaf pans.

11. Cover. Allow dough to rise for 1 hour, or until dough has doubled in size.

12. Bake at 350°F for 30 minutes.

13. When done baking, brush tops of loaves with melted butter.

Whole Wheat Bread

Makes: 3 loaves
Prep Time: 30 minutes
Standing Time: 1 hour
Rising Time: 2–4 hours
Baking Time: 35 minutes

2½ tablespoons dry active yeast
2½ cups warm (110–112°F) water, *divided*
1 tablespoon sugar
4 teaspoons salt
2 cups whole wheat flour
½ cup brown sugar
½ cup water
½ cup vegetable oil or lard, melted
½ cup molasses or honey
4–5 cups white flour

1. In a large bowl, dissolve yeast in 2 cups water.

2. Add sugar, salt, and whole wheat flour. Mix well.

3. Let stand for 1 hour.

4. Add brown sugar, ½ cup water, oil, and molasses. Stir together.

5. Add white flour until dough is smooth and elastic.

6. Cover with a towel or plastic wrap and let rise for 1 hour, or until dough is double in size.

7. With fists, punch down dough.

8. Shape dough into 3 loaves and place in well-greased loaf pans.

9. Cover. Let dough rise for 1 hour, or until dough is double in size.

10. Bake at 350°F for 35 minutes.

TIP:
For faster rising time, place the covered bowl in the oven. Keep oven off. The warmth of the pilot light helps dough rise faster.

Potato Rolls

Makes: 12 rolls
Prep Time: 30 minutes
Rising Time: 3–3½ hours
Baking Time: 15–20 minutes

1 cup warm (110–112°F) water
1 tablespoon dry active yeast
½ cup vegetable oil
1 cup mashed potatoes
½ cup sugar
2 eggs
½ teaspoon salt
5–5½ cups Occident,* *or* all-purpose, flour

Occident flour is bread flour made from western wheat

1. In a small bowl, mix water and yeast.

2. Let stand 15 minutes.

3. In a large bowl, stir together oil, mashed potatoes, sugar, eggs, and salt.

4. Add yeast mixture.

5. Stir in flour and knead until smooth. Dough will be sticky.

6. Cover and let rise for 2 hours.

7. Using hands, shape dough into rolls.

8. Place in a well-greased cake pan or cupcake pan. Cover. Let rise for 1–1½ hours, or until dough has doubled in size.

9. Bake at 350°F until rolls are golden brown, about 15–20 minutes.

Dinner Rolls

Makes: 12–18 rolls
Prep Time: 30 minutes
Cooling Time: 30–45 minutes
Rising Time: 2–4 hours
Baking Time: 20–30 minutes

2 tablespoons dry active yeast
½ cup warm (110–112°F) water
1 cup milk
1 tablespoon salt
½ cup sugar
8 tablespoons (1 stick) butter, melted
2 eggs, beaten
5½ cups flour, *divided*
Melted butter for top

1. Dissolve yeast in warm water and let stand.

2. In a medium pan, heat milk until almost boiling.

3. Add salt, sugar, and butter to milk.

4. Cool milk mixture until lukewarm, 80–85°F.

5. Stir in yeast mixture and eggs.

6. Add flour, stirring in as much as you can until well mixed.

7. Knead in remaining flour, or as much as you can, until dough is smooth and elastic.

8. Place dough in a well-greased bowl. Cover and let rise for 1–2 hours, or until dough is double in size.

9. Form dough into rolls and place on a well-greased cookie sheet or jelly-roll pan, approximately 2" apart.

10. Cover. Allow dough to rise for 1–2 hours, or until dough is double in size.

11. Bake at 350°F for 20–30 minutes, until rolls are light brown.

12. Brush tops of rolls with melted butter before taking off cookie sheet.

Quick Cinnamon Rolls

Makes: 2 large pans
Prep Time: 20–40 minutes
Rising Time: 30–60 minutes
Baking Time: 25–35 minutes

Prepared bread dough, enough to make 2 loaves
Butter at room temperature
Cinnamon

Sauce:
1 cup cream
1 cup corn syrup
½ cup honey
1½ cups brown sugar
8 tablespoons (1 stick) butter

TIP:
Refrigerator bread works well for these rolls (see page 10).

1. Roll out bread dough ¼"–½" thick.

2. Spread dough with butter and sprinkle with cinnamon.

3. Starting with long side, roll up dough.

4. Slice rolled dough into pieces about 1" thick.

5. Place sliced dough into well-greased baking pans. Cover and let rise for ½–1 hour, or until dough has doubled in size.

6. Bake at 350°F for 20–30 minutes until golden brown on top.

7. To make sauce, boil cream, corn syrup, honey, brown sugar, and butter for 5 minutes.

8. When cinnamon rolls are finished baking, pour sauce over rolls in pans.

9. Return to the oven for 5 minutes.

10. Serve warm.

Cinnamon Rolls

Makes: 4–5 round cake pans full
Prep Time: 45–60 minutes
Cooling Time: 30–45 minutes
Rising Time: 2–3½ hours
Baking Time: 15–20 minutes

1½ cups milk
16 tablespoons (2 sticks) butter, cut in chunks
1 cup warm (110–112°F) water
4 tablespoons dry active yeast
½ cup sugar
4 eggs, beaten
2 teaspoons salt
8 cups flour, *divided*

Topping:
1 cup (2 sticks) butter, melted
½ cup brown sugar
1–2 teaspoons cinnamon

1. In a large saucepan, heat milk until almost boiling.

2. Stir in butter until dissolved.

3. Cool until lukewarm, 80–85°F.

4. When cooled, add water, yeast, sugar, eggs, and salt.

5. Beat in 1–3 cups of flour.

6. Add rest of flour, kneading well.

7. Cover and let rise until doubled, 1–1½ hours.

8. Roll out dough to approximately ½" thick.

9. Brush with melted butter. Sprinkle with brown sugar and cinnamon.

10. Starting with the long side, roll up dough.

11. Cut the dough into slices that are 1" thick.

12. Place cut dough in a well-greased pan and allow to rise for 1–2 hours or until double in size.

13. Bake at 350°F until golden brown, about 15–20 minutes.

14. Cool slightly, but frost while still warm (see Frosting for Cinnamon Rolls, page 14).

Pumpkin Bread

Makes: 2 loaves
Prep Time: 15 minutes
Baking Time: 1 hour

3 cups sugar
1 cup vegetable oil
4 eggs
2 cups pumpkin
3½ cups flour
1 teaspoon baking powder
1 teaspoon baking soda
1 teaspoon salt
½ teaspoon cloves
1 teaspoon cinnamon
1 teaspoon nutmeg
⅔ cup water

1. In a medium bowl, combine sugar, oil, eggs, and pumpkin.

2. In a separate bowl, combine flour, baking powder, baking soda, salt, cloves, cinnamon, and nutmeg.

3. Add dry ingredients to sugar mixture. Stir well.

4. Add water and stir to combine.

5. Pour batter into 2 well-greased loaf pans.

6. Bake at 350°F for approximately 1 hour, or until toothpick inserted in center of loaves comes out clean.

TIP:
Always check bread before time is up. Bread may be done sooner than 1 hour.

Zucchini Bread

Makes: 2 loaves
Prep Time: 15 minutes
Baking Time: 1 hour

3 eggs
2 cups sugar
1 cup vegetable oil
2 cups grated zucchini
1 tablespoon vanilla extract
1 teaspoon salt
1 tablespoon cinnamon
1 teaspoon baking soda
¼ teaspoon baking powder
3 cups flour
1 cup chopped nuts, *optional*

1. In a large bowl, combine eggs, sugar, and oil.

2. Stir in zucchini.

3. Add remaining ingredients in order given, except nuts. Stir well.

4. Add nuts if you wish.

5. Pour batter into 2 well-greased loaf pans.

6. Bake at 325°F for 1 hour, or until toothpick inserted in center of loaves comes out clean.

7. Cool before removing from pan.

TIP:
If zucchini is big and has tough skin, peel before grating. If using young, slender zucchini, there is no need to peel.

Breakfast Dishes

Creamed Eggs

Makes: 6–8 servings
Prep Time: 15 minutes
Cooking Time: 5 minutes

2 tablespoons (¼ stick) butter
2 tablespoons flour
1 teaspoon salt
Dash black pepper
2 cups milk
6 hard-boiled eggs
6–8 slices toast

1. Melt butter in a medium saucepan.
2. Stir in flour, salt, and pepper.
3. Stirring constantly, slowly add milk.
4. Cook until smooth and slightly thickened. Remove from the heat.
5. Peel eggs. Slice or chop.
6. Stir into white sauce.
7. Serve over toast or Cornmeal Mush (see page 38).

TO HARD-BOIL EGGS:

1. Place eggs in a saucepan. Cover with water.
2. Bring to a full, rolling boil.
3. Turn off burner.
4. With lid on, let eggs stand for 10 minutes.
5. Cool immediately under cold running water.
6. Peel and serve.

Dutch Eggs

Makes: 8 servings
Prep Time: 15 minutes
Baking Time: 45 minutes

8 eggs
2½ cups milk
5 tablespoons flour
½ teaspoon baking powder
½–1 teaspoon salt

1. In a medium bowl, beat eggs and milk together.

2. Add flour, baking powder, and salt. Mix well.

3. Pour mixture into a well-greased 2-quart casserole dish.

4. Bake at 350°F for 45 minutes.

Breakfast Casserole

Makes: 6–8 servings
Prep Time: 45 minutes
Chilling Time: 2–3 hours
Baking Time: 45 minutes
Standing Time: 10 minutes

6–8 medium potatoes, peeled or unpeeled
8 eggs
2 teaspoons water
¾ teaspoon salt
¼ teaspoon pepper
3 cups sharp cheese, grated

1. Cook potatoes until medium-soft. They should still be slightly crunchy. Cool to room temperature.

2. Refrigerate for 2 hours to make shredding easier.

3. After chilling, shred potatoes and place in the bottom of a greased 9"×13" baking dish.

4. In a separate bowl, beat eggs, water, salt, and pepper together.

5. Pour egg mixture over potatoes and sprinkle with cheese.

6. Bake at 350°F for 30 minutes, covered. Take off cover and continue baking for 15 minutes.

7. Let stand for 10 minutes before serving.

VARIATIONS:

Add more vegetables by adding green peppers or onion to the egg mixture in Step 4.

Sprinkle cooked ham, bacon, or sausage over mixture before adding cheese in Step 5.

Creamed Dried Beef

Makes 4 — 6 servings
Prep Time: 10 minutes
Cooking Time: 20 minutes

2 teaspoons butter
¼ pound chipped dried beef
¼ cup flour
3 cups milk
1 teaspoon chopped onion
½ teaspoon Worcestershire sauce, optional

1. Melt butter in a deep skillet.

2. Stir in chipped beef and cook for 5 minutes.

3. Sprinkle flour over beef and stir to coat evenly.

4. Stirring constantly, slowly pour in milk.

5. Add onion and Worcestershire sauce if you wish.

6. Cook over medium heat until thickened.

7. Serve chipped beef over biscuits, toast, stewed crackers or fried mush. (See recipe for Cornmeal Mush on page 38.)

TIP:
Add more flour to thicken creamed dried beef in step 3 if you wish.

Tomato Gravy

Makes: 4–6 servings
Prep Time: 3 minutes
Cooking Time: 10 minutes

1 cup tomato juice
5 tablespoons flour
¼ teaspoon salt
Dash pepper
2 cups milk

1. Pour tomato juice into a medium saucepan and bring to a boil.

2. In a separate bowl, combine flour, salt, pepper, and milk to form a smooth paste.

3. Pour flour mixture into hot tomato juice, stirring constantly.

4. Heat until thickened.

5. Serve tomato gravy over Cornmeal Mush (recipe on page 38), fried potatoes, or eggs and toast.

Sausage Gravy

Makes: 8–10 servings
Prep Time: 2 minutes
Cooking Time: 20–25 minutes

4 tablespoons (½ stick) butter
2 pounds bulk sausage
1¼ cups flour
½ teaspoon salt
¼ teaspoon pepper
2 quarts milk

1. Melt butter in a large saucepan.

2. Brown sausage in butter, stirring to break up clumps and cooking until pink is gone.

3. Add flour, salt, and pepper slowly by sprinkling over sausage and stirring constantly.

4. Still stirring, slowly add milk.

5. Mixture will thicken. If mixture gets thicker than you'd like, add more milk.

6. Serve over biscuits or toast.

Oatmeal Pancakes

Makes: 8–10 pancakes
Prep Time: 5 minutes
Cooking Time: 2–5 minutes

1 cup dry quick oatmeal
1 cup whole wheat flour
2 eggs
½ cup sour cream
½–¾ cup milk, until batter is the consistency you like
1 teaspoon baking soda
1 teaspoon vinegar

1. In a medium bowl, combine dry oatmeal and flour.

2. Stir in eggs, sour cream, and milk.

3. In a separate bowl, dissolve baking soda in vinegar.

4. Stir baking soda mixture into batter.

5. Spoon batter onto hot skillet.

6. Fry pancakes until golden brown on both sides.

TIP:
Thin batter will make thin pancakes. Thicker batter will make thicker pancakes.

French Toast

Makes: 4 servings
Prep Time: 5 minutes
Cooking Time: 10–15 minutes

1 egg
⅓ cup milk
½ teaspoon cinnamon
4 slices homemade bread
2–4 tablespoons melted butter
Syrup

1. With an egg beater, beat egg, milk, and cinnamon.

2. Pour mixture into a shallow bowl.

3. Dip bread into egg mixture, one slice at a time, being sure to soak both sides.

4. Fry in melted butter until golden brown on each side.

5. Serve with syrup.

Cornmeal Mush

Makes: 4 servings
Prep Time: 5 minutes
Chilling Time: 4–6 hours, or overnight

3 cups water
1 cup cornmeal
1 teaspoon salt
Vegetable oil

1. Stir together water, cornmeal, and salt in a saucepan. Over medium heat, continue stirring until mixture comes to a boil.

2. Turn heat to low and simmer for 20 minutes.

3. Pour into a loaf pan and chill for 4–6 hours, or overnight.

4. When chilled, cut into ¼"-thick slices

5. Fry in oil until golden brown and crispy. Flip to brown both sides.

VARIATION:
Mush is delicious with fried eggs and ketchup.

Chicken and Turkey Dishes

Crispy Baked Chicken

Makes: 6–8 servings
Prep Time: 20 minutes
Baking Time: 1–1½ hours

¾ cup cornflakes
1 ½ teaspoons salt
¼ teaspoon pepper
1 egg, beaten
3 pounds chicken legs and thighs
8 tablespoons (1 stick) butter

1. Crush cornflakes to make crumbs in a shallow bowl.

2. Add salt and pepper.

3. Beat egg in a separate shallow bowl.

4. Line a roaster, or 9"×13" baking pan, with aluminum foil.

5. Dip chicken in egg, and then cornflake mixture.

6. Place in the pan lined with aluminum foil.

7. Melt butter and drizzle over chicken.

8. Bake uncovered at 350°F for 1–1½ hours, or until juice runs clear when chicken is pricked with a fork.

Fried Chicken

Makes: 5 servings
Prep Time: 20 minutes
Baking Time: 1–1½ hours

1 cup flour
2 teaspoons salt
½ teaspoon pepper
3 pounds chicken legs and thighs
4 tablespoons (½ stick) butter

1. Place flour, salt, and pepper in a shallow bowl or pan. Mix well.

2. Dip each piece of chicken in seasoned flour until well coated.

3. In a large skillet, melt butter.

4. Carefully place floured chicken in melted butter. Fry chicken in batches rather than crowd chicken. If the skillet is too full, the chicken will steam and not brown.

5. Fry until golden brown on both sides.

6. Line a cake pan or jelly-roll pan with aluminum foil.

7. Transfer browned chicken to pan.

8. Bake uncovered at 350°F for 1–1½ hours or until tender.

This perfectly crispy fried chicken was a tradition in my family, served with my mother's Ohio Filling. Since Ohio was her native state, she simply called it "dressing." The chicken was served on heaping platters when I was a child, and is now served the same way at our Christmas dinners. It's the son-in-laws' favorite.

Chicken Gumbo

Makes: 10–12 servings
Prep Time: 30 minutes
Baking Time: 30–45 minutes

9 slices bread, toasted and cubed
4 cups cooked and cubed chicken
4 tablespoons (½ stick) butter, melted
½ cup Miracle Whip salad dressing
4 eggs, beaten
1 cup chicken broth
1 cup milk
1 teaspoon salt
2 (10¾-ounce) cans cream of celery soup
9 slices cheese of your choice

1. Place bread cubes in the bottom of a greased 9"×13" baking dish.

2. Sprinkle chicken over top.

3. In a separate bowl, combine melted butter, Miracle Whip, eggs, broth, milk, salt, and soup.

4. Pour mixture over chicken.

5. Top with cheese.

6. Bake at 350°F for 30–45 minutes, or until lightly browned.

Roasting a Chicken

Makes: 6–8 servings
Prep Time: 15 minutes
Roasting Time: About 20 minutes per pound, plus 10–20 minutes extra

1 small to medium roasting chicken
Butter, at room temperature
Salt
½ cup water

1. Using hands, rub butter on chicken, inside and out.

2. Sprinkle salt liberally on outside.

3. Place chicken in a small roaster or pan of your choice.

4. Add water.

5. Bake uncovered at 425°F for 20 minutes, and then reduce heat to 375°F for remaining time.

TIP:
Calculate about 20 minutes per pound, plus 10–20 minutes more. A good thermometer should register 165°F in the center of the chicken when the chicken is fully cooked.

Chicken or Beef Gravy

Makes: 4 servings
Prep Time: 5 minutes
Cooking Time: 15 minutes

1 pint broth with meat drippings if available
2–3 tablespoons flour
¼ teaspoon salt
Dash pepper
1 cup water

1. Heat broth until boiling.

2. In a separate bowl, mix flour, salt, and pepper. Stir in water to make a smooth paste.

3. Add to broth and stir.

4. Heat until thickened, stirring continually.

5. Stir in the cooked chicken or beef. Serve over mashed potatoes, noodles, rice, or toast points.

TIP:
You can add as much or as little flour-water paste to the broth to make it as thick or thin as you like.

Roascht or Chicken Filling

Makes: 15 servings
Prep Time: 45 minutes
Baking Time: 1½–2 hours

8 tablespoons (1 stick) butter
2 cups chopped celery
2 loaves bread, cubed
3 cups cooked and diced chicken
6 eggs, beaten
1 teaspoon salt
Pepper to taste

1. Melt butter in a large skillet.

2. Add celery and sauté until soft.

3. Toss bread and chicken together in a large bowl.

4. Pour celery and eggs over bread mixture.

5. Sprinkle with salt and pepper and mix well.

6. Pour into a greased roaster or large baking dish.

7. Bake uncovered at 350°F for 1½–2 hours.

8. During baking time, stir occasionally, stirring bread away from sides of pan to prevent burning.

Ohio Filling

Makes: 15 servings
Prep Time: 1 hour
Baking Time: 1½–2 hours

1 cup chopped celery
½ cup diced potatoes
½–1 cup chopped carrots
2 loaves bread, cubed
1 cup (2 sticks) butter, melted
6 eggs, beaten
5–6 cups milk
1 cup chicken broth
1 tablespoon chicken bouillon
½ teaspoon pepper
1 teaspoon seasoned salt
2 tablespoons parley, fresh or dried
2 cups cooked and diced chicken

1. In a saucepan, cook celery, potatoes, and carrots over medium heat, in about 1" of water, until tender.

2. In a large bowl, toss bread cubes with melted butter.

3. Spread bread cubes onto 2 baking sheets.

4. Toast at 375°F in the oven for 20 minutes, or until nicely browned.

5. In a large mixing bowl, combine eggs, milk, broth, bouillon, pepper, seasoned salt, and parsley.

6. Add chicken, celery, potatoes, carrots, and toasted bread cubes. Mix gently.

7. Pour into a large greased roaster or 1 or 2 baking pans.

8. Bake uncovered at 350°F for 1½–2 hours.

9. Stir occasionally.

10. Serve when top is brown and crusty.

Turkey Bake

Makes: 6–8 servings
Prep Time: 30 minutes
Baking Time: 40 minutes

8 slices bread, cubed, *divided*
2 cups cooked, cubed turkey
2 cups shredded cheese
¼ cup chopped onion
1 tablespoon butter
2 cups milk
3 eggs
½ teaspoon salt
¼ teaspoon pepper

1. Place half of bread cubes in a well-greased 9"×9" baking pan or casserole dish.

2. Spread turkey over bread.

3. Sprinkle cheese over turkey.

4. In a small skillet, sauté onion in butter.

5. Spread onion over cheese.

6. Cover with remaining bread cubes.

7. In a separate bowl, stir milk, eggs, salt, and pepper together.

8. Pour over casserole.

9. Bake at 350°F for 40 minutes.

NOTE:
This casserole is almost a quick version of *Roascht* (see page 49).

Meats and Other Main Dishes

Laura's Scalloped Oysters

Makes: 6 servings
Prep Time: 20 minutes
Baking Time: 40–45 minutes

5 cups Ritz crackers
½ cup butter
½ teaspoon salt
Pepper
1 pint shucked small oysters
1 cup cream
¼ teaspoon Worcestershire sauce

1. Preheat the oven to 375°F.

2. Combine crackers with butter, salt, and pepper.

3. Put ⅓ crumbs in bottom of a 9"×13" casserole dish. Arrange half of oysters on top. Top with ⅓ crumbs, then more oysters, and then the final layer of crumbs.

4. Drizzle evenly with cream and Worcestershire sauce.

5. Bake for 40–45 minutes or until browned on top.

Our oldest daughter Laura must have inherited her grandmother's love of cooking, as usually her recipes turn out great, whereas I tend to flounder around in the kitchen. This recipe is easy to make, and just wonderful, and has become an established tradition since she introduced it. The oyster flavor shines through the richness of the other ingredients.

Ground Beef Casserole

Makes: 8–10 servings
Prep Time: 45–60 minutes
Baking Time: 30–35 minutes

2 pounds ground beef
1 small onion, chopped
3 teaspoons salt, *divided*
2 (10¾-ounce) cans tomato soup
1½ quarts home-canned or 3 (15½-ounce) cans, green beans
9 medium potatoes
1 egg
¼ teaspoon pepper
½ cup warm milk
4 tablespoons (½ stick) butter, optional

1. Brown ground beef, onion, and 2 teaspoons salt in a skillet until cooked and crumbly.

2. Drain off drippings.

3. In a large bowl, combine ground beef, tomato soup, and green beans.

4. Pour into a greased 9"×13" baking dish.

5. Peel, cook, and mash potatoes.

6. When potatoes are mashed, add egg, 1 teaspoon salt, pepper, milk, and butter if you wish.

7. Spread potatoes over ground beef mixture.

8. Bake at 350°F for 30–35 minutes.

Meat Loaf

Makes: 8 servings
Prep Time: 30 minutes
Baking Time: 1 hour

For Meat Loaf:
1½ pounds ground beef
¾ cup dry quick oats
1 egg, beaten
¾ cup milk
1½ teaspoons salt
¼ cup chopped onion
¼ teaspoon pepper

For Sauce:
½ cup ketchup
2 tablespoons brown sugar
1 tablespoon prepared mustard

1. Combine meat loaf ingredients in the order given.

2. With clean hands, mix well. Shape into loaf.

3. Place in a well-greased pan.

4. Combine sauce ingredients and pour on top.

5. Bake at 350°F for 1 hour.

Hot Roast Ground Beef

Makes: 6–8 servings
Prep Time: 30 minutes
Baking Time: 1–3 hours

1 pound ground beef
⅔ cup tomato juice
½ cup dry bread crumbs
¼ cup ketchup
1 teaspoon salt
2 teaspoons Worcestershire sauce
¼ teaspoon pepper
6–8 medium potatoes, sliced ½-¾" thick
4–6 medium carrots, sliced
1 large onion, sliced
Parsley
Salt and pepper to taste

1. In a large bowl, combine ground beef, tomato juice, bread crumbs, ketchup, salt, Worcestershire sauce, and pepper.

2. Mix well.

3. Shape into loaf.

4. Place into a large, greased casserole dish or roaster.

5. Add potatoes, carrots, and onion in layers around meat loaf.

6. Sprinkle with parsley, salt, and pepper.

7. Bake at 300°F for 2–3 hours, or at 375°F for 1–1½ hours.

Ground Beef Gravy

Makes: 8–10 servings
Prep Time: 20 minutes
Cooking Time: 20 minutes

2 pounds ground beef
2 small onions, chopped
1 teaspoon salt
¼ teaspoon pepper
½ cup flour
3 cups milk
10¾-ounce can cream of mushroom soup, optional
12-ounce can evaporated milk, optional

1. In a large skillet, brown ground beef, onions, salt, and pepper.

2. Cook, stirring frequently until no pink remains and meat is crumbly.

3. Stir in flour.

4. Remove from the heat and stir in milk.

5. Return to medium heat.

6. Add soup and evaporated milk, if using.

7. Cook, stirring frequently until smooth and thickened.

8. Serve over mashed potatoes.

Poor Man's Steak

Makes: 4–5 servings
Prep Time: 20 minutes
Chilling Time: 8–10 hours, or overnight
Baking Time: 45 minutes

1 pound ground beef
1 cup cracker crumbs or dry oatmeal
1 small onion, chopped
1 teaspoon salt
¼ teaspoon pepper
1 cup milk
2 tablespoons (¼ stick) butter
10¾-ounce can cream of mushroom soup

1. In a large bowl, mix ground beef, cracker crumbs, onion, salt, pepper, and milk.

2. Shape into loaf.

3. Refrigerate for 8–10 hours, or overnight.

4. Remove from the refrigerator and slice into ½"-thick slices.

5. Brown each slice in butter in a skillet.

6. Place browned slices in a greased 9"×13" baking pan.

7. Cover with soup.

8. Bake at 350°F, covered, for 45 minutes.

VARIATION:
Substitute gravy for cream of mushroom soup, if you wish.

Barbecued Ham Slices

Makes: 12–16 servings
Prep Time: 20 minutes
Baking Time: 2 hours

1 tablespoon butter
¼ cup chopped onion
½ cup ketchup
⅓ cup water
2 tablespoons brown sugar
1 tablespoon Worcestershire sauce
2 tablespoons white vinegar
12 slices boneless ham

1. Melt butter in a medium saucepan.

2. Add onion and cook until soft.

3. In a separate bowl, combine ketchup, water, brown sugar, Worcestershire sauce, and vinegar.

4. Add to the saucepan with onions and bring to a boil.

5. Simmer for 5 minutes.

6. Arrange ham slices in a single layer in a large greased casserole dish (or dishes) or roaster.

7. Pour sauce over ham.

8. Bake at 350°F for 1½ hours. Baste occasionally with sauce.

Old-Fashioned Baked Ham

Makes: 10–15 servings
Prep Time: 30 minutes
Baking Time: 70–75 minutes

5-pound ham
½ cup brown sugar
¼ teaspoon ground cloves, optional
1 teaspoon dry mustard
1 tablespoon vinegar
8-ounce can pineapple slices, with 2 tablespoons
   juice reserved
12–20 maraschino cherries, optional

1. Bake ham, uncovered, in a roaster at 350°F for 30 minutes.

2. While ham is baking, combine brown sugar, cloves, mustard, vinegar, and 2 tablespoons pineapple juice to make glaze.

3. Remove ham from the oven and score.

4. Place pineapple, and cherries if you wish, on top of ham.

5. Spoon glaze over fruit and ham.

6. Bake for another 40–45 minutes, basting occasionally.

CHURCH SERVICES

At Christmastime, the ministers always preach the same chapter in the *Schrift* (Bible) about Jesus's birth. At lunch, instead of the usual schnitz pie, there are Christmas cookies on platters with mint tea served along with coffee, so the children have a hot drink with their cookies. There is often a more festive air, children looking forward to the opening of presents at home.

Christmas trees are *verboten* (not allowed), as are extensive decorating and outdoor lighting, but each family has bits of garland, wreaths, candles, and holly in their homes. Brightly wrapped Christmas presents are in every household.

Ham Loaf

Makes: 8–10 servings
Prep Time: 30 minutes
Baking Time: 1 ½ hours

For Ham Loaf:
1 pound ground ham
1 pound bulk sausage
2 cups soft bread crumbs
2 eggs, beaten
1 cup sour cream
1 teaspoon dry mustard
⅛ teaspoon paprika
⅛ teaspoon black pepper

For Sauce:
½ cup packed brown sugar
½ cup pineapple juice
1 tablespoon Clear-Jel, or cornstarch

1. In a large bowl, mix all ham loaf ingredients.

2. Form into a loaf and place in greased loaf pan.

3. Bake uncovered at 350°F for 1 hour.

4. While ham loaf is baking, prepare sauce.

5. Combine ingredients for sauce in a small pan.

6. Bring to a boil. Stir frequently over medium heat until smooth and thickened.

7. When ham loaf has baked for an hour, remove from the oven.

8. Drain ham loaf drippings into prepared sauce.

9. Baste ham loaf with sauce.

10. Return to the oven and bake 30 more minutes, or until lightly browned.

Green Bean and Sausage Casserole

Makes: 6–8 servings
Prep Time: 45 minutes
Baking Time: 30 minutes

1–1½ pounds bulk pork sausage
1 quart home-canned or 2 (15½-ounce) cans, green beans
6 medium-sized potatoes
¾ cup water
¼ pound grated cheddar cheese
10¾-ounce can cream of mushroom soup

1. Brown sausage in a skillet, stirring frequently to break up clumps until no pink remains.

2. Drain off drippings.

3. Place sausage in a large mixing bowl.

4. Drain green beans. Add to mixing bowl with meat.

5. Peel and cut potatoes into cubes.

6. Place cubed potatoes in a saucepan with ¾ cup water.

7. Cover. Cook over low to medium heat until tender. Stir frequently to prevent sticking. Add more water if needed so potatoes don't cook dry.

8. When fully cooked, drain and add to meat and green beans in bowl.

9. Stir together well.

10. Pour into a greased 9"×13" baking dish.

11. Add cheese and soup. Stir to combine.

12. Bake at 350°F for 30 minutes.

Sausage Potato Casserole

Makes: 8–10 servings
Prep Time: 30 minutes
Baking Time: 70–80 minutes

1 pound bulk pork sausage, *divided*
10¾-ounce can cream of mushroom soup
¾ cup milk
¼ cup chopped onion
½ teaspoon salt
½ teaspoon pepper
½ teaspoon parsley
3 cups raw potatoes, sliced thinly, *divided*
1 cup shredded cheese

1. In a large skillet, brown sausage. Stir frequently to break up clumps and until no pink remains. Drain off drippings.

2. In a separate bowl, mix soup, milk, onion, and seasonings.

3. In a casserole dish, layer half the potatoes, then sausage, then soup mixture.

4. Repeat layers until ingredients are all used.

5. Cover and bake at 350°F until potatoes are tender, about 60–70 minutes.

6. Remove from the oven and sprinkle with cheese.

7. Return to the oven, uncovered, until cheese is melted, about 10 more minutes.

Baked Macaroni and Cheese

Makes: 6 servings
Prep Time: 30 minutes
Baking Time: 30 minutes

1 ½ cups uncooked macaroni
5 tablespoons butter, *divided*
3 tablespoons flour
1 ½ cups milk
1 cup shredded cheddar cheese
½ cup cubed American cheese
½ teaspoon salt
¼ teaspoon pepper
2 tablespoons dried bread crumbs

1. Cook macaroni according to directions on package.

2. Drain and put in greased 2-quart baking dish.

3. In a medium saucepan, melt 4 tablespoons butter.

4. Add flour and stir until smooth.

5. Stirring constantly, slowly pour in milk.

6. Boil for 2 minutes, stirring continually.

7. Reduce heat to medium.

8. Stir in cheeses, salt, and pepper.

9. Pour over macaroni and mix well.

10. In a separate saucepan, melt remaining butter.

11. Add bread crumbs and brown lightly.

12. Sprinkle bread crumbs over macaroni.

13. Bake uncovered at 350°F for 30 minutes.

Floating Islands

Makes: 6–8 servings
Prep Time: 15 minutes
Baking Time: 20–30 minutes

1 pound hot dogs
6 cups mashed potatoes
½–¾ pound cheese, cut in long, narrow strips
Sauerkraut, optional

1. Heat hot dogs in a saucepan until warm in center.

2. Remove from the pan and cut a slit down the length of each hot dog.

3. Fill with mashed potatoes.

4. Place cheese on top of potatoes.

5. Place hot dogs on a cookie sheet or jelly-roll pan.

6. Bake at 350°F for 20–30 minutes, or until well browned.

VARIATION:
Sauerkraut goes well with Floating Islands. Heat the sauerkraut in a separate saucepan.

Salads

Broccoli and Cauliflower Salad

Makes: 10–12 servings
Prep Time: 30 minutes
Chilling Time: 2–3 hours

1 head broccoli
1 head cauliflower
½ pound shredded cheddar cheese
½–1 pound bacon, fried crisp and crumbled
1 cup chopped onions, optional

Dressing:
1 cup Miracle Whip salad dressing
1 cup sour cream
½ cup sugar
½ teaspoon salt
1–2 teaspoons vinegar

1. Chop broccoli and cauliflower into bite-sized pieces. Place in a large bowl.

2. Stir in cheese, bacon, and onions if you wish.

3. In a separate bowl, combine dressing ingredients. Add vinegar to suit your taste.

4. Pour dressing over chopped vegetables.

5. Cover. Refrigerate for at least 2 hours before serving.

Lettuce with Cream Dressing

sometimes called "Cream Lettuce"

Makes: 6–8 servings
Prep Time: 15–20 minutes

8 cups leaf lettuce or baby lettuce, fresh from the garden
2 hard-boiled eggs, optional

Dressing:
½ cup sugar
¼ cup vinegar
⅓–½ cup sour cream
2–3 tablespoons sliced green onions

1. Wash and dry lettuce. Place lettuce in a large bowl.

2. Slice eggs and add to lettuce if you wish.

3. In a separate bowl, combine dressing ingredients.

4. Just before serving, pour dressing over lettuce. Toss to coat.

Layered Green Salad

Makes: 10–12 servings
Prep Time: 30 minutes
Chilling Time: 6–8 hours, or overnight

1 head iceberg lettuce, chopped
1 cup chopped celery
4 hard-boiled eggs, sliced or grated
8 slices cooked bacon, crumbled
1-pound bag frozen peas
1 cup shredded carrots
2 cups mayonnaise
1 cup shredded cheese of your choice

1. In a 9"×13" pan, make a layer of lettuce, followed by a layer of celery, a layer of eggs, a layer of bacon, a layer of peas, and a layer of carrots.

2. Spread mayonnaise over vegetables.

3. Sprinkle cheese on top.

4. Do not toss! Cover.

5. Refrigerate for 6–8 hours, or overnight.

6. Toss before serving, or serve layered.

Carrot-Raisin Salad

Makes: 4–5 servings
Prep Time: 20 minutes

2½ cups shredded carrots (approximately
   3 large carrots)
½ cup chopped celery
½ cup raisins
½ cup mayonnaise
1 teaspoon lemon juice

1. In a medium bowl, mix carrots, celery, and raisins.

2. In a small bowl, mix mayonnaise and lemon juice.

3. Pour dressing over salad ingredients and mix gently but well.

4. Cover. Refrigerate until ready to serve.

Cucumber and Onion Salad

Makes: 4 servings
Prep Time: 20 minutes

2 large cucumbers, sliced, and peeled if you wish
1 large onion, sliced
¾ cup sour cream
3 tablespoons vinegar
2 tablespoons sugar
Dash salt
Dash pepper

1. Combine cucumbers and onion in good-sized mixing bowl.

2. In a separate bowl, mix sour cream, vinegar, sugar, salt, and pepper.

3. Pour dressing over cucumbers and onions. Mix well.

4. Cover and refrigerate until ready to serve.

Coleslaw

Makes: 8–10 servings
Prep Time: 30–45 minutes
Chilling Time: 2–3 hours

1 large head cabbage, shredded
1 cup chopped celery
½ medium onion, chopped
1 green bell pepper, chopped

Dressing:
1½ cups sugar
½–¾ cup vinegar
1 teaspoon celery seed
½ teaspoon mustard seed
2 teaspoons salt

1. In a large bowl, mix cabbage, celery, onion, and pepper.

2. In a separate bowl, stir together sugar, vinegar, celery seed, mustard seed, and salt.

3. Stir dressing into vegetables.

4. Cover. Refrigerate for 2–3 hours before serving to allow flavors to blend.

Creamy Coleslaw

Makes: 4–6 servings
Prep Time: 30 minutes
Chilling Time: 2–3 hours

½ head cabbage, shredded
2 carrots, grated
2 tablespoons parsley

Dressing:
¼ cup vinegar
¼ cup sugar
½ cup mayonnaise
2 teaspoons celery seed

1. Place cabbage, carrots, and parsley in a medium bowl.

2. In a separate bowl, mix vinegar, sugar, mayonnaise, and celery seed.

3. Add dressing to vegetables. Stir.

4. Cover and refrigerate for 2–3 hours to allow flavors to blend.

Potato Salad

Makes: 6–8 servings
Prep Time: 30 minutes
Cooking Time: 20 minutes
Chilling Time: 4 hours for potatoes; 3–4 hours, or overnight, for completed salad

6 medium to large potatoes, unpeeled
4–6 hard-boiled eggs, grated
½ cup chopped celery
¼–½ cup chopped onion

Dressing:
1½ cups mayonnaise
¾ cup sugar
¼ cup milk
⅛ cup vinegar
3 tablespoons prepared mustard
2 teaspoons salt

1. Boil potatoes until slightly soft, but not too soft. Drain.

2. Chill potatoes until completely cold, to make grating easier.

3. Peel. Grate cold potatoes into good-sized mixing bowl.

4. Gently fold in grated hard-boiled eggs and chopped celery and onion.

5. In a separate bowl, combine dressing ingredients and mix well.

6. Pour dressing over potato mixture. Stir to combine.

7. Cover. Chill for 3–4 hours, or overnight, and then serve.

Macaroni Salad

Makes: 4 servings
Prep Time: 20 minutes
Cooking Time: 8–10 minutes
Chilling time: 3–4 hours, or overnight

2 heaping cups uncooked macaroni
½ cup grated carrots
½ cup diced celery
2 hard-boiled eggs, chopped
¼ cup chopped onions
1 teaspoon parsley

Dressing:
1 cup mayonnaise
1 tablespoon prepared mustard
½ teaspoon salt
1 tablespoon vinegar

1. Cook macaroni according to package directions.

2. Drain. Cool in a large mixing bowl.

3. Add carrots, celery, eggs, onion, and parsley to macaroni in mixing bowl.

4. In a separate bowl, stir together mayonnaise, mustard, salt, and vinegar.

5. Combine dressing with pasta and vegetables.

6. Cover. Refrigerate for 3–4 hours, or overnight, before serving.

Red Beet Eggs

Makes: 12 servings
Prep Time: 30 minutes
Chilling Time: 24 hours

12 eggs
1 quart pickled red beets

1. To make hard-boiled eggs, place eggs in a saucepan. Cover with water.

2. Bring to a full, rolling boil.

3. Turn off the burner.

4. With the lid on, let eggs stand for 10 minutes.

5. Cool immediately under cold running water.

6. Peel eggs. Place in a large bowl. (Eggs should remain whole.)

7. Pour quart of red beets, with juice, over peeled eggs.

8. Cover. Refrigerate for 24 hours before serving. Eggs will turn a deep rose color.

Christmas Salad

Makes: 12–15 servings
Prep Time: 20 minutes
Chilling Time: 7–8 hours, total

Layer 1:
4 cups boiling water
2 (3.4-ounce) packages
  lime gelatin
15-ounce can crushed
  pineapple, drained but
  with juice reserved

Layer 2:
2 envelopes Dream Whip
  topping mix
8-ounce package cream
  cheese, softened to
  room temperature

Layer 3:
1½ cups pineapple juice
3 eggs
1 cup sugar
3 tablespoons flour
Pinch salt
Lettuce leaves

1. To make the first layer, bring water to a boil in a medium saucepan.

2. Stir gelatin into boiling water.

3. Place the saucepan containing dissolved gelatin in the refrigerator. Allow to chill until just starting to set.

4. Drain crushed pineapple, saving juice.

5. Stir drained pineapple into chilled, partially set gelatin.

6. Pour mixture into a 9"×13" pan. Cover and return to the refrigerator until stiff.

7. To make the second layer, mix whipped topping according to package directions.

8. Add cream cheese in chunks to whipped topping, stirring until smooth.

9. When gelatin is firm, spread layer of whipped topping/cream cheese mixture on top.

10. Cover and return gelatin to the refrigerator so second layer can firm up.

11. For the third layer, add water to reserved pineapple juice so it equals 1½ cups.

12. Separate the eggs. (Save whites for another use.)

13. Combine pineapple juice, sugar, egg yolks, flour, and salt in a medium saucepan. Cook over medium heat, stirring constantly, until thickened.

14. When first two layers of salad are firm, spread third layer on top.

15. Refrigerate for 2–3 hours, or until all three layers are firm, before serving.

16. Cut into squares. Place lettuce leaves on individual salad plates. Top each with a square of Christmas Salad.

Apple Salad

Makes: 6–8 servings
Prep Time: 30 minutes
Cooling Time: 20 minutes
Cooking Time: 5–10 minutes

20-ounce can crushed pineapple
2 eggs, beaten
1 ½ cups sugar
2 tablespoons flour
2 tablespoons (¼ stick) butter, cut into chunks
1 teaspoon vinegar
1 teaspoon vanilla extract
6–8 peeled apples, chopped or grated
3 bananas, sliced

1. To make the dressing, drain pineapple and reserve the juice.

2. Add water to pineapple juice to equal 2 cups.

3. Combine pineapple juice, eggs, sugar, and flour in a medium saucepan.

4. Cook until thickened, stirring continually to prevent sticking.

5. Stir in butter, vinegar, and vanilla.

6. Allow to cool.

7. In a separate bowl, combine apples, bananas, and pineapple.

8. Pour dressing over fruit and stir to combine.

9. Cover and chill until ready to serve.

Jell-O Mold

Makes: 8 servings
Prep Time: 20 minutes
Cooling Time: 30–45 minutes
Chilling Time: approximately 3 hours

1 cup water
2 (3.4-ounce) packages gelatin, any flavor
8-ounce package cream cheese, softened
12-ounce can evaporated milk
8-ounce container frozen whipped topping, thawed

1. Bring water to a boil in a small saucepan.

2. Dissolve gelatin in boiling water.

3. Cool to room temperature.

4. In a large bowl, beat cream cheese until creamy. Stir in evaporated milk until well blended.

5. Fold in whipped topping.

6. Mix cooled gelatin with creamy mixture.

7. Pour into a gelatin mold or into individual serving dishes.

8. Refrigerate for 3 hours, or until firm.

Vegetables

Baked Corn

Makes: 4–6 servings
Prep Time: 15 minutes
Baking Time: 40–45 minutes

2 eggs
2 cups corn
1 cup milk
⅔ cup crushed cracker crumbs
3 tablespoons butter, melted
½ teaspoon salt
¼ teaspoon, or less, pepper
1 tablespoon sugar
¼ cup minced onion

1. In a small bowl, beat eggs.

2. In a separate bowl, combine all other ingredients.

3. Add eggs and mix well.

4. Pour into a 1½-quart greased casserole dish. Bake at 350°F for 40–45 minutes, or until a knife inserted in the center of the dish comes out clean.

Green Bean Casserole

Makes: 6 servings
Prep Time: 20 minutes
Baking Time: 40 minutes

2 (16-ounce) packages frozen green beans
10¾-ounce can cream of chicken, celery, or
   mushroom soup
½ cup milk
⅛ teaspoon pepper
2 (8-ounce) cans French-fried onions, optional

1. Cook green beans in a small amount of water, covered, for approximately 10 minutes in a saucepan. Drain. Green beans will be slightly crunchy.

2. In a large bowl, mix soup, milk, and pepper until smooth. Stir in beans.

3. Place mixture into a greased 2- to 2½-quart baking dish.

4. Sprinkle with onions.

5. Bake at 350°F for 40 minutes.

Corn Fritters

Makes: 4 servings
Prep Time: 10 minutes
Cooking Time: 10–15 minutes

2 cups fresh corn, thawed frozen corn, or canned
  corn, drained well
2 eggs
¼ cup flour
1 teaspoon salt
⅛ teaspoon pepper
1 teaspoon baking powder
2 teaspoons cream
½ cup vegetable oil
Confectioners' sugar, optional

1. In a medium bowl, combine corn, eggs, flour, salt, pepper, and baking powder.

2. Stir in cream.

3. Pour vegetable oil into a large skillet.

4. When oil is hot, drop teaspoonfuls of corn mixture into oil.

5. Fry until golden brown and crispy on both sides.

6. Before serving, sprinkle with confectioners' sugar if you wish.

Corn on the Cob

Makes: 4 ears of corn
Prep Time: 10 minutes
Cooking Time: 15 minutes

4 ears of fresh corn, husked and silked

1. Place ears of corn in an 8–10 quart stockpot.
2. Cover corn with cold water.
3. Cover pot. Bring water to a boil.
4. Boil uncovered for 2–5 minutes, depending on the size of the ears and their kernels.
5. Turn the burner off and let the corn stand in hot water for 10 minutes.

Barbecued Green Beans

Makes: 6–8 servings
Prep Time: 20 minutes
Baking Time: 1–1½ hours

½ pound bacon
¼ cup chopped onion
¾ teaspoon salt
½ cup sugar
¾ cup ketchup
¾ teaspoon Worcestershire sauce
4 cups fresh or canned green beans

1. Cut bacon into bite-sized pieces.

2. Place bacon and onion in a medium skillet. Fry until bacon is crispy.

3. Remove bacon and allow to drain.

4. In a separate bowl, stir together browned onion, salt, sugar, ketchup, and Worcestershire sauce.

5. Add beans and bacon and mix well.

6. Pour into a greased 3- to 3½-quart baking dish.

7. Cover. Bake at 300°F for 1–1½ hours. (Fresh beans will require a longer cooking time than canned beans. Check after 1 hour to see if beans are as tender as you like them.)

Barbecued Beans

Makes: 6–8 servings
Prep Time: 30 minutes
Baking Time: 1 hour

2 medium onions, chopped
2 tablespoons (¼ stick) butter
1 tablespoon vinegar
2 tablespoons brown sugar
1 tablespoon flour
1 cup ketchup
1 cup cut-up, cooked ham or 8 slices bacon, cooked crisp and crumbled, optional
2 (15½-ounce) cans or 4 cups home-canned great northern or navy beans, undrained

1. Cook onions in butter in a skillet until soft. Remove from the heat.

2. In a large bowl, mix vinegar, brown sugar, flour, and ketchup.

3. Stir onions into sauce.

4. Add ham or bacon if you wish.

5. Add beans and mix well.

6. Pour into a greased 2-quart baking dish.

7. Cover and bake for 45 minutes at 350°F.

8. Uncover. Bake for an additional 15 minutes.

TIP:
If sauce seems too thick in step 2, add extra ketchup.

Cooked Celery

Makes: 4 servings
Prep Time: 10 minutes
Cooking Time: 20 minutes

1 ½ cups chopped celery
1 tablespoon butter
1 tablespoon flour
1 tablespoon sugar
1 tablespoon vinegar
1 egg, beaten
½ cup water

1. Place celery in a medium saucepan.

2. Cover celery with water and cook until soft. Drain off water. Set celery aside.

3. In a separate saucepan, melt butter.

4. Stir in flour, sugar, and vinegar.

5. Cook slowly until mixture starts to boil.

6. Reduce heat and allow to simmer a few minutes.

7. Add beaten egg and water.

8. Allow to boil lightly until slightly thickened.

9. Stir thickened sauce into celery and serve.

Crusty Baked Potatoes

Makes: 6 servings
Prep Time: 15 minutes
Baking Time: 1 hour

6 medium potatoes
1 cup crushed cracker crumbs
4 tablespoons (½ stick) butter, melted
1 teaspoon seasoned salt

1. Peel potatoes. Rinse and cut in half.

2. In a shallow dish, combine cracker crumbs and melted butter.

3. Grease a 9"×13" baking dish.

4. Roll potatoes halves in cracker crumbs until well coated.

5. Place potatoes in a baking dish, cut-side up.

6. Sprinkle with seasoned salt.

7. Bake at 350°F for 1 hour, or until soft.

Scalloped Potatoes

Makes: 10–12 servings
Prep Time: 30 minutes
Cooking Time: 30–40 minutes
Baking Time: 1 hour

8–10 medium potatoes
1 medium onion, chopped
4 tablespoons (½ stick) butter
2–3 cups milk
¾–1 teaspoon salt
¼ teaspoon pepper
1 cup water
1 tablespoon flour
1 cup shredded cheese of your choice

1. Peel potatoes and cook in water over medium heat until medium soft, but allow for a little crunch.

2. Meanwhile, grease a 9"×13" baking dish.

3. When potatoes are cool, slice into a greased baking dish.

4. In a medium saucepan, cook onion in butter until soft.

5. Add milk to onions.

6. Add salt and pepper.

7. In a separate bowl, stir water and flour into a smooth paste.

8. Add flour mixture to onion mixture. Over medium heat, stir continually until sauce becomes creamy and thickened.

9. Remove from the heat and stir in cheese until melted.

10. Pour sauce over potatoes and mix.

11. Bake at 350°F for 1 hour.

Mashed Potatoes

Makes: 4–6 servings
Prep Time: 10 minutes
Cooking Time: 30 minutes

4–6 large potatoes
1–1 ½ cups milk
1 teaspoon salt
4 tablespoons (½ stick) butter
8-ounce package cream cheese, softened, or 1 cup
    sour cream, optional
1–1 ½ cups milk

1. Peel potatoes and cut into large pieces.

2. Place potatoes in a saucepan. Add about 2" of water. Cover.

3. Bring to a boil over medium heat. Reduce heat, but allow potatoes and water to simmer, cooking until potatoes are very soft. Check to make sure potatoes do not cook dry.

4. While potatoes are cooking, place milk in a saucepan. Heat just to boiling point, but do not boil. A skin will form when the milk gets as hot as it should be.

5. Drain water from cooked potatoes.

6. Mash potatoes with potato masher or wire whisk.

7. Add salt and butter and continue mashing.

8. Add cream cheese or sour cream if you wish and continue mashing.

9. Add milk until potatoes are creamy.

Zucchini Casserole

Makes: 6–8 servings
Prep Time: 15–20 minutes
Baking Time: 45 minutes

3 eggs
¼ cup vegetable oil
½ cup flour
½ teaspoon salt
1 ½ teaspoons baking powder
½ cup grated cheese of your choice
¼ cup parsley
½ cup chopped onion
2 cups unpeeled grated zucchini

1. In a medium bowl, beat eggs and oil together.

2. Stir in flour, salt, and baking powder.

3. Add cheese, parsley, onion, and zucchini.

4. Mix well.

5. Pour into a greased 2-quart casserole dish. Bake at 350°F for 45 minutes.

Sweet Potato Casserole

Makes: 6 servings
Prep Time: 15 minutes
Cooking Time: 20–30 minutes
Baking Time: 35–45 minutes

3 medium to large sweet potatoes, peeled
2 eggs
½ cup milk
¼ cup sugar
½ teaspoon salt
4 tablespoons (½ stick) butter, melted
½ teaspoon vanilla extract

Crumbs:
½ cup sugar
1 cup chopped nuts
⅓ cup flour
⅓ stick butter, melted

1. Cook potatoes in a saucepan in about 2" water, covered, until very tender.

2. Drain potatoes. Mash until smooth.

3. In a large mixing bowl, mix eggs, milk, sugar, salt, butter, and vanilla.

4. Stir potatoes into egg mixture.

5. Spoon into a greased 2-quart baking dish.

6. To make crumbs, combine sugar, nuts, flour, and butter in a small bowl.

7. Sprinkle crumbs over potatoes.

8. Bake at 350°F for 35–45 minutes, or until heated through.

Desserts

Apple Crumb Pie

Makes: 1 9" pie, or 8 slices
Prep Time: 25 minutes
Baking Time: 40 minutes

1½ cups water
1 cup brown sugar
1 teaspoon cinnamon
1 tablespoon cornstarch
1 tablespoon butter, softened
2–3 cups grated apples
9" unbaked piecrust (see recipe for Piecrust on page 128)

Crumbs:
1 cup brown sugar
1 cup dry oatmeal
½ cup flour
3 tablespoons butter

1. In a medium saucepan, combine water, brown sugar, cinnamon, and cornstarch. Cook over medium heat, stirring frequently until smooth and slightly thickened.

2. Remove the saucepan from the heat. Stir in butter and apples.

3. Pour into unbaked piecrust.

4. To make the crumbs, stir brown sugar, oatmeal, and flour together in a good-sized mixing bowl.

5. Using a pastry cutter or 2 forks, cut butter into mixture until small crumbs form.

6. Sprinkle crumbs evenly over pie.

7. Bake at 425°F for 10 minutes.

8. Reduce heat to 350°F and continue baking for 30 minutes.

Peach Pie

Makes: 1 9" pie, or 8 slices
Prep Time: 15–20 minutes
Cooling Time: 20–30 minutes
Baking Time: 30–40 minutes

¾ cup sugar
¼ teaspoon salt
2 tablespoons Clear-Jel
⅓ cup water
1 quart peaches, peeled and cut into bite-size pieces
1 9" unbaked piecrust with top crust (see recipe for Piecrust on page 128)

1. In a small bowl, combine sugar, salt, Clear-Jel, and water. Mix well.

2. Place peaches in a medium saucepan over low to medium heat.

3. When peaches are hot, gently stir in Clear-Jel mixture.

4. Continue heating, stirring continually, until mixture comes to a boil. Allow to cook until thickened, continuing to stir.

5. Cool until warm but not hot.

6. Pour into unbaked piecrust.

7. Roll out crust to top pie. Lift over filled pie and pinch edges to secure. Cut 6 slashes across top crust to allow steam to escape.

8. Bake at 425°F for 10 minutes.

9. Reduce heat to 375°F and continue baking for 20–30 minutes, or until filling is bubbly and crust is browned.

Blueberry Pie

Makes: 1 9" pie, or 8 slices
Prep Time: 15–20 minutes
Cooling Time: 2–3 hours
Baking Time: 40 minutes

¾–1 cup sugar
¼ teaspoon salt
2 tablespoons Clear-Jel
½ cup water
1 quart blueberries, fresh or canned
9" unbaked 2-layer piecrust (see page 128 for Piecrust recipe)

1. In a small bowl, combine sugar, salt, Clear-Jel, and water.

2. Drain blueberries (unless using fresh berries). Pour berries into medium saucepan and heat.

3. When berries are hot, gently stir in Clear-Jel mixture.

4. Continue heating until the mixture boils and thickens slightly.

5. Cool to room temperature.

6. Pour into unbaked piecrust.

7. Roll out remaining pastry to make pastry lid for pie. Place on top of pie. Cut slits to allow steam to escape.

8. Bake at 425°F for 10 minutes.

9. Reduce heat to 375°F. Continue baking for 30 minutes, or until blueberry filling is bubbly and top crust is well browned.

Pumpkin Pie

Makes: 2 9" pies, or 16 slices
Prep Time: 20 minutes
Baking Time: 40 minutes

1¼ cups sugar
1 tablespoon flour
1½ teaspoons cinnamon
½ teaspoon salt
3 eggs, separated
1¼ cups canned pumpkin
12-ounce can evaporated milk
1½ teaspoons vanilla extract
1½ cups milk, heated
2 9" unbaked piecrusts

1. In a medium bowl, combine sugar, flour, cinnamon, and salt.

2. Using 2 other bowls, separate eggs.

3. Add yolks to the sugar mixture. Stir with a whisk.

4. Stir in pumpkin.

5. Add evaporated milk and vanilla.

6. Heat 1½ cups milk on stove, stirring constantly until milk is hot, but not boiling.

7. With a wire whisk, slightly beat egg whites.

8. Add milk and egg whites to the pumpkin mixture and stir.

9. Divide evenly between 2 unbaked piecrusts.

10. Bake at 425°F for 10 minutes.

11. Reduce heat to 350°F and continue baking for 30 minutes.

12. Remove from the oven when pie is still slightly shaky in the middle.

13. Cool to room temperature before slicing and serving.

Butterscotch Pie

Makes: 2 9" pies, or 16 slices
Prep Time: 20–25 minutes
Cooling Time: 1 hour
Chilling Time: 3–4 hours

1st part:

1 cup brown sugar
3 tablespoons butter
1 cup water
1 teaspoon vanilla extract
¼ teaspoon baking soda
¼ teaspoon salt

2nd part:

1 cup brown sugar
3 tablespoons flour
3 tablespoons cornstarch
3 eggs
4½ cups milk
2 9" baked piecrusts (see page 128 for Piecrust recipe)

1. To make the first part of the pie, place brown sugar and butter into a good-sized saucepan. Bring to a boil, stirring constantly.

2. Boil mixture for 5 minutes, continuing to stir.

3. Remove from the heat and add water.

4. Stir in vanilla, baking soda, and salt. Set aside.

5. To make the second part of the pie, stir together brown sugar, flour, cornstarch, and eggs in a separate bowl.

6. Gradually add milk, whisking constantly so that mixture is smooth.

7. Add second part to the first part in the saucepan. Over medium heat, cook, stirring constantly, until mixture is thickened.

8. Pour into baked piecrusts.

9. Cool to room temperature. Then cover and refrigerate for 3–4 hours, or until butterscotch filling is set and can be sliced.

Shoofly Pie

Makes: 2 9" pies, or 16 slices
Prep Time: 20 minutes
Baking Time: 1 hour

Crumbs:

3 cups pastry flour
¾ cup brown sugar
½ teaspoon baking soda
½ teaspoon baking powder
8 tablespoons (1 stick) butter, at room temperature

Gooey Bottom:

1½ cups brown sugar
1 small egg
1 cup sweet molasses
1½ cups hot water
½ teaspoon baking soda
2 9" unbaked piecrusts

1. To make the crumbs, stir flour, brown sugar, baking soda, and baking powder together in a good-sized mixing bowl.

2. Using a pastry cutter or 2 forks, cut butter into mixture.

3. Stir with a fork until mixture forms soft crumbs.

4. Using another mixing bowl, stir together all ingredients for the gooey bottom.

5. Stir 2 cups crumbs into gooey bottom mixture. (Reserve remaining crumbs.)

6. Divide gooey bottom mixture between 2 unbaked piecrusts.

7. Sprinkle evenly with reserved crumbs.

8. Bake at 400°F for 15 minutes.

9. Reduce heat to 350°F and continue baking for 45 minutes.

Schnitz Pie

Makes: 1 9" pie, or 8 slices
Prep Time: 30–40 minutes
Cooking Time: 45 minutes

3 cups dried apples
2¼ cups warm water
1 teaspoon lemon extract
⅔ cup brown sugar
9" unbaked piecrust, plus top crust

1. Soak apples in the warm water until plump and filled out.

2. Place apples and any remaining water in a saucepan. Cover and cook until very soft.

3. Mash apples. Add lemon extract and sugar, stirring well.

4. Pour into unbaked piecrust.

5. Cover with top crust. Seal edges.

6. Bake at 425°F for 15 minutes. Turn oven to 350°F and continue baking for 30 more minutes.

NOTE:
Schnitz Pie is served each Sunday at the lunch following the church service. This pie can be made year-round; it doesn't depend on seasonal fruit. It can also be made in advance, an important advantage since the family hosting church in their home usually serves 75–100 people.

Chocolate Pie

Makes: 2 9" pies, or 16 slices
Prep Time: 15 minutes
Chilling Time: 3–4 hours

1¼ cups sugar

2 teaspoons vanilla extract

8-ounce package cream cheese, softened

¾ cup milk

½ cup dry baking cocoa

16-ounce container frozen whipped topping, thawed (+ more, if you want to serve some on top of pie, too)

2 9" baked piecrusts (see page 128 for Piecrust recipe)

1. In an electric mixer bowl, combine sugar and vanilla.

2. Add cream cheese in chunks, beating thoroughly after each addition.

3. Stir in milk and baking cocoa.

4. Fold in whipped topping.

5. Divide mixture between 2 baked piecrusts.

6. Chill in the refrigerator for 3–4 hours, so pie sets up and holds its shape when cut.

7. If you wish, top with dollops of whipped cream on each slice when serving.

Mom Kauffman's Pecan Pie

Makes: 3 9" pies
Prep Time: 20 minutes
Baking Time: 50 minutes
Chilling Time: 2 hours

2 cups brown sugar
3 tablespoons flour
2 cups Green Label Karo (Karo Pancake Syrup)
1 ½ cups water
12 tablespoons (1 ½ stick) butter, melted
3 teaspoons vanilla extract
9 well-beaten eggs
3 cups pecans
3 bottom piecrusts, unbaked

1. Preheat the oven to 350°F.

2. Combine all ingredients (except piecrusts), adding eggs and pecans last. Mix thoroughly and pour into three bottom piecrusts.

3. Bake for about 50 minutes or until filling is set (it shouldn't be very jiggly when you remove it from the oven).

4. Allow to cool for at least 2 hours or overnight.

This pie has been served at every Christmas dinner since I was very small. It is very rich, complete with a thick layer of crunchy pecans on top.

Jigglers

Makes: about 15 pieces, depending on size of molds.
Prep Time: 10 minutes
Chilling Time: 3 hours

⅔ cup Jell-O gelatin
1 ½ cups boiling water

1. Stir together the Jell-O gelatin and boiling water and pour into molds.

2. Chill for at least 3 hours.

3. To unmold, dip the bottoms of the molds in warm water for a few seconds and then invert onto a plate.

Everyone makes Jigglers, but not always do they come in the perfectly shaped Christmas stars and bells. Red or green, the children love a glassy Jiggler on their plate when they sit down to eat at the Christmas table. But the best part is knowing there are plenty more to eat in the afternoon.

Reindeer Munch

Makes: about 15 cups
Prep Time: 20 minutes

3 cups Rice Chex or Corn Chex
3 cups Cheerios
3 cups pretzels
3 cups peanuts
3 cups M&Ms
20 ounces white chocolate

1. Combine the cereals, pretzels, peanuts, and M&Ms.

2. Melt the white chocolate, pour over cereal mixture, and stir.

An Amish tradition is to have a large Christmas dinner with every member of the family present, followed by all kinds of snacks and beverages in the afternoon and until late in the evening. Every family has their own special homemade "party mix" recipe, so I started one, or so I hoped, with this sweet and salty combination. I was proud to present it in an attractive bowl, but it was largely ignored, for no fair reason. My children are special, prone to wrinkling noses at new things. This recipe is not mine. This one comes from my friend Rosanne Rissler.

Chocolate Whoopie Pies

Makes: 4 dozen whoopie pies
Prep Time: 1 hour
Baking Time: 8–10 minutes

2 cups sugar
1 cup vegetable oil
2 eggs
4 cups flour
1 cup dry baking cocoa
1 teaspoon salt
1 cup buttermilk
2 teaspoons vanilla extract
2 teaspoons baking soda
1 cup hot water

1. Combine sugar, oil, and eggs in a large mixing bowl. Beat until creamy.

2. Sift together flour, dry cocoa, and salt.

3. Add dry ingredients to creamed mixture alternately with buttermilk.

4. Stir in vanilla.

5. In a separate bowl, whisk baking soda and hot water together until soda is dissolved.

6. Stir into batter until thoroughly mixed.

7. Drop by rounded teaspoonfuls onto well-greased baking sheets.

8. Bake at 400°F for 8–10 minutes. To avoid dry whoopie pies, do not overbake.

9. Remove from sheets and allow to cool completely.

10. Spread filling (see recipe on page 134) on flat side of one cookie. Top with second cookie.

11. To store, wrap each whoopie pie in plastic wrap.

Whoopie Pie Filling

Makes: 6 cups, enough for 2 dozen whoopie pies
Prep Time: 5 minutes

2 egg whites, beaten
4 cups confectioners' sugar, *divided*
1 teaspoon vanilla extract
1 ½ cups Crisco

1. Mix egg whites, 2 cups sugar, and vanilla.

2. Beat in Crisco and remaining sugar.

3. Spread on flat side of whoopie pie "cookie." Top with second cookie. Be sure to use plenty of filling for each cookie.

Pumpkin Whoopie Pies

Makes: 2–3 dozen whoopie pies
Prep Time: 30 minutes
Baking Time: 10–15 minutes

2 cups brown sugar
1 cup vegetable oil
1 ½ cups canned pumpkin
3 cups all-purpose flour
1 teaspoon baking powder
1 teaspoon baking soda
1 teaspoon cinnamon
½ teaspoon ground ginger

1. In a large bowl, combine brown sugar, oil, and canned pumpkin until well mixed.

2. Stir in remaining ingredients, mixing well.

3. Drop by teaspoonfuls on well-greased baking sheets.

4. Bake at 375°F for 10–15 minutes, or until a toothpick inserted in the center of a cookie comes out clean.

5. Remove from the cookie sheets and allow to cool.

6. Spread whoopie pie filling (see Filling recipe on page 134) on flat side of a cookie. Top with a second cookie, making a "sandwich."

7. To store, wrap each cookie in plastic wrap.

Grandmother's Buttermilk Cookies

Makes: 125 cookies
Prep Time: 30 minutes
Baking Time: 10–12 minutes

3 pounds sugar
1 pound lard
4 eggs
4 pounds flour
2 tablespoons baking soda
1 tablespoon cream of tartar
1 quart buttermilk
1 cup walnuts
Confectioners' sugar

1. Preheat the oven to 350°F.

2. Cream together sugar and lard. Add eggs and mix.

3. In a separate bowl, whisk together flour, baking soda, and cream of tartar.

4. Add to lard mixture alternately with buttermilk, mixing until fully combined. Add walnuts and mix.

5. Use a soup spoon to drop on greased cookie sheet, spacing cookies about 2 inches apart.

6. Bake for 10–12 minutes, or until edges are just turning brown. Cool on wire racks. When cool, shake in bag with confectioners' sugar until covered.

This recipe is from my grandmother ("Mommy" is the Dutch word for grandmother). Very large families (in Mommy's case, fourteen children) required very large recipes. My mother used to fill a lard can with these, with the cookies stacked in layers with waxed paper in between. I can still taste the soft, rounded cookie with half-melted confectionary sugar soaked through. They were a staple in our pantry, a quick snack. My parents had six children in six years, a pair of twins among us. When they were born, Sunday company ate their way through a whole lard can of these cookies.

Raspberry Jam Strips

Makes: about 64 pieces
Prep Time: 1 hour 15 minutes
Baking Time: 10–12 minutes

1 cup butter, softened
⅓ cup sugar
⅓ cup brown sugar
1 egg
1½ teaspoons vanilla extract, *divided*
2½ cups flour
1 teaspoon baking powder
½ cup raspberry jam
1 cup confectioners' sugar
2 teaspoons water

1. Cream together butter, sugar, and brown sugar. Add egg and 1 teaspoon vanilla and mix. Stir in flour and baking powder.

2. Chill dough for at least one hour.

3. Preheat the oven to 350°F. Divide dough into 8 parts and, on an ungreased cookie sheet, roll each into an 8-inch rope.

4. Press each rope flat until 1½ inches wide, then make an indentation down the length of each. Fill the indentations with jam.

5. Bake for 10–12 minutes, or until lightly browned along the edges. Cool completely.

6. Mix the confectioners' sugar, ½ teaspoon vanilla, and water and drizzle in a zigzag over the strips.

7. Slice diagonally in 1-inch pieces.

These make any tray of cookies look very attractive, with the purple raspberry jam in the middle of the bar, with a drizzle of white frosting. My daughters and I just love these.

Cranberry Cookies

Makes: 4 dozen cookies
Prep Time: 30 minutes
Baking Time: 10–12 minutes

½ cup butter, softened
1 cup sugar
¾ cup brown sugar
1 egg
¼ cup milk
2 tablespoons orange juice
3 cups flour
1½ teaspoons baking powder
¼ teaspoon baking soda
½ teaspoon salt
1 cup chopped nuts
1 cup vanilla chips
2 cups dried cranberries

1. Preheat the oven to 375°F. Grease a baking sheet or line with parchment paper.

2. Cream together butter, sugar, and brown sugar. Add egg and milk and mix until fully combined. Stir in orange juice.

3. In a separate bowl, combine flour, baking powder, baking soda, and salt. Add the wet ingredients to the dry and mix to combine.

4. Fold in nuts, vanilla chips, and cranberries.

5. Drop by rounded teaspoonful onto a cookie sheet, spacing them about 2 inches apart, and bake for 10–12 minutes or until the edges are lightly browned. Transfer cookies to a wire rack to cool.

The brown butter icing on these is the perfect sweet accompaniment to the tangy cranberries. These will probably remain a Christmas tradition for the grandchildren for years to come.

Susan Martin's Date Balls

Makes: 3 dozen cookies
Prep Time: 15 minutes

2 cups chopped dates
2 cups sugar
½ cup butter
4 eggs lightly beaten
1 teaspoon salt
½ cup nuts, chopped
4 cups Rice Krispies

1. In a medium saucepan, combine the first five ingredients and cook over medium heat for about 5 minutes.

2. Remove from the heat and stir in nuts and cereal. Cool, shape into balls, and roll in coconut.

Our son Andy tasted these Date Balls somewhere years before I attempted to make them. I thought they'd be difficult—cooking a candy mixture to the proper "stage" is terrifying. To my surprise, these are easy to make and absolutely delicious, especially for coconut lovers.

Never-Fail Fudge

Makes: 16 pieces
Prep Time: 15 minutes

⅓ cup butter

4½ cups sugar

1 (14.5-ounce) can Carnation evaporated milk

1 cup marshmallow crème

20 ounces Hershey's milk chocolate bars, chopped into small pieces

1 (12-ounce) package chocolate chips

2 teaspoons vanilla extract

2 cups nuts

1. Grease a 9-inch square baking pan.

2. Combine butter, sugar, and evaporated milk. Boil for 5½ minutes, stirring well (burns easily).

3. Remove from the heat and stir in marshmallow crème, chocolate pieces, and chocolate chips until fully melted. Stir in vanilla and nuts. Pour into the pan and cool completely before cutting into small squares.

Ridiculously simple to make, this fudge is the creamiest and is a Christmas staple. Stacked in small squares on a plate beside a plate of Rice Krispie Candy (what we call Rice Krispie Treats), it is delicious, eaten in small bites that melt on your tongue. My mother always brought it out in the afternoon, after gifts were exchanged at the Christmas dinner.

Ginger Cookies

Makes: 4 dozen cookies
Prep Time: 20 minutes
Baking Time: 10–12 minutes

2 cups sugar
1½ cups oil
2 eggs
½ cup light molasses
4 cups flour
4 teaspoons baking soda
1 tablespoon ginger
2 teaspoons cinnamon
1 teaspoon salt
2 cups white chocolate chips
1 tablespoon Crisco

1. Preheat the oven to 350°F.

2. Cream together sugar, oil, eggs, and molasses. In a separate bowl, whisk together flour, baking soda, ginger, cinnamon, and salt.

3. Mix wet and dry ingredients. Roll into balls and then roll balls in sugar.

4. Place on an ungreased cookie sheet about 2 inches apart and bake for 10–12 minutes. Cool completely.

5. In a double boiler, melt and stir together white chocolate chips and Crisco. Use a spoon to drizzle a little over each cookie.

A close friend and neighbor, Lucy Zimmerman, made dozens of cookie platters for Christmas, to sell. These are among my favorites.

Chocolate Chip Cookies

Makes: 4 dozen cookies
Prep Time: 30 minutes
Baking Time: 8–10 minutes

3 cups brown sugar
1½ cups vegetable oil
4 eggs
3½-ounce box instant vanilla pudding
1 teaspoon salt
2 teaspoons vanilla extract
4½ cups all-purpose flour, *divided*
1½–2 cups chocolate chips

1. In a large bowl, combine brown sugar, vegetable oil, and eggs. Stir until thoroughly combined.

2. Stir in pudding mix, salt, and vanilla, again until well combined.

3. Add flour 1 cup at a time, mixing well after each addition of flour.

4. Stir in chocolate chips.

5. Drop by teaspoonfuls onto a greased cookie sheet.

6. Bake at 350°F for 8–10 minutes, or until cookies are golden brown around the edges.

TIP:
Do not overbake these very soft cookies.

Peanut Butter Chocolate Chip Cookies

Makes: 7–8 dozen cookies
Prep Time: 30 minutes
Baking Time: 8–10 minutes

2 cups flour
1 teaspoon baking soda
½ teaspoon salt
1 cup granulated sugar
1 cup brown sugar
1 cup shortening or 1 cup (2 sticks) butter, softened
2 eggs
1 teaspoon vanilla extract
1 cup creamy peanut butter
1 cup chocolate chips
1 cup chopped, unsalted peanuts, optional

1. Sift flour, baking soda, and salt together in a medium-sized bowl. Set aside.

2. In a large mixing bowl, cream together sugars and shortening.

3. Add eggs and vanilla to creamed mixture. Beat until fluffy.

4. Stir in peanut butter.

5. Add sifted ingredients and mix well.

6. Stir in chocolate chips and peanuts if you wish.

7. Drop by teaspoonfuls onto well-greased cookie sheets.

8. Bake at 350°F for 8–10 minutes.

Chocolate Chip Cookie Bars

Makes: 24 bars
Prep Time: 20 minutes
Baking Time: 25 minutes

⅔ cup (1 stick + 2⅔ tablespoon) butter, softened
1½ cups brown sugar
½ cup granulated sugar
3 eggs
1 teaspoon vanilla extract
2 cups flour
1 teaspoon baking powder
½ teaspoon salt
1 cup chocolate chips
½ cup chopped pecans, optional

1. In a large bowl, cream together butter and sugars.

2. Beat in eggs and vanilla.

3. Stir in flour, baking powder, and salt.

4. Add chocolate chips and pecans if you wish.

5. Spread in a well-greased 12"×15" jelly-roll pan.

6. Bake at 350°F for 25 minutes.

7. When bars have cooled, cut with a plastic knife (which makes smoother edges for the bars than a metal knife).

Butterscotch Nut Cookies

Makes: about 7 dozen cookies
Prep Time: 20 minutes
Chilling Time: 2–3 hours
Baking Time: 8–10 minutes

2 cups brown sugar
2 eggs
1 cup (2 sticks) butter, softened
1 teaspoon vanilla extract
3½ cups flour
1 teaspoon baking soda
1 teaspoon cream of tartar
1 cup chopped walnuts or pecans

1. In a large mixing bowl, combine brown sugar, eggs, and butter.

2. Add vanilla and beat until thoroughly combined.

3. Stir in flour, baking soda, cream of tartar, and nuts until well blended.

4. Shape dough into logs about 2" around. (If dough is too soft to handle, chill in the refrigerator for 1 hour, and then try again.)

5. Wrap each log in plastic wrap. Chill for at least 2 hours.

6. Unwrap dough and slice into ¼"-thick pieces.

7. Lay slices flat on a well-greased cookie sheet. Allow about 1" between slices.

8. Bake at 350°F for 8–10 minutes.

GRISCHTAG SINGIN'

The Christmas hymn singing is another time-honored tradition. Each Amish community has their different districts of twenty to thirty-five families, but at Christmastime, the entire community is invited to one hymn singing.

Hosted in a large garage or shop, church benches and folding chairs placed appropriately, the cadence reaches to the rafters, with hundreds of voices melding together in songs of praise.

The old German Christmas carols are printed in the *Gesang-Buch*, a brown, thinner version of the *Ausbund*. Modern-day tunes are fitted to these *Grischtag lieda*, so each one is a rousing rendition of the Christmas carols we know, fitted to German words.

There is always food afterward, everyone bringing Christmas cookies, snacks, cheese, meat, or other delicacies. Gallons of coffee and hot chocolate are put in Styrofoam cups and distributed among the crowd. It is a blessed time of togetherness and rejoicing in the birth of our Savior.

Molasses Cookies

Makes: 4 dozen cookies
Prep Time: 30–40 minutes
Baking Time: 10–12 minutes

1½ cups vegetable oil
2 cups brown sugar
2 eggs
¾ cup molasses (Brer Rabbit is best!)
4 teaspoons baking soda
½ teaspoon salt
1 teaspoon ground ginger
2 teaspoons ground cinnamon
5 cups all-purpose flour, *divided*
1 cup granulated sugar

1. In a large bowl, combine oil, brown sugar, and eggs, mixing well.

2. Stir in molasses until well blended.

3. Add baking soda, salt, ginger, and cinnamon, mixing well.

4. Add flour 1 cup at a time, mixing thoroughly after each addition of flour. The dough will be stiff.

5. Place granulated sugar into a shallow bowl or plate.

6. Using a teaspoon, scoop out dough and roll into a small ball. Roll the unbaked cookie in granulated sugar.

7. Place cookies on well-greased cookie sheets.

8. Flatten slightly with the back of a spoon before baking.

9. Bake at 350°F for 10–12 minutes.

Grandpa Cookies

Makes: 10 dozen cookies
Prep Time: 30 minutes
Baking Time: 12–15 minutes

1 cup (2 sticks) butter, softened
3 cups brown sugar
5 eggs
1 cup sour cream
4¾ cups flour
1 tablespoon baking soda
1 tablespoon baking powder

1. Cream butter and sugar in a large bowl.

2. Add eggs and sour cream. Beat well.

3. Add remaining ingredients and stir to combine.

4. Drop by teaspoonfuls onto well-greased cookie sheets.

5. Bake at 375°F for 12–15 minutes.

6. Frost with Caramel Frosting (see recipe on page 160) or Creamy Jelly Roll Topping (see recipe on page 164).

Sand Tarts

Makes: 4–5 dozen cookies
Prep Time: 30–45 minutes
Chilling Time: 6–8 hours, or overnight
Baking Time: 8–10 minutes

1 cup (2 sticks) butter, softened
3 cups brown sugar
4 eggs, *divided*
1 teaspoon vanilla extract
4 cups all-purpose flour
1 teaspoon cream of tartar
1 teaspoon baking soda
Sugar, cinnamon, and/or sprinkles for topping

1. In a large bowl, cream butter and sugar together.

2. Add 3 eggs and vanilla. Reserve 1 egg for topping.

3. Stir in flour, cream of tartar, and baking soda.

4. Roll dough into ball and wrap in plastic wrap. Chill for 6–8 hours, or overnight.

5. Roll out chilled dough so that it is ¼" thick.

6. Using cookie cutters, cut out dough. Place on greased baking sheets, about 1" apart.

7. In a small bowl, beat 1 egg. Using a pastry brush, brush the tops of the cookies with the beaten egg.

8. Sprinkle cookies with sugar, cinnamon, and/or sprinkles.

9. Bake at 350°F for 8–10 minutes.

Chocolate Cake

Makes: 9 × 13 pan
Prep Time: 15 minutes
Baking Time: 20–30 minutes

¾ cup vegetable oil
2 cups granulated sugar
3 eggs
2½ cups flour
¾ cup dry baking cocoa
2 teaspoons baking powder
2 teaspoons baking soda
1 cup buttermilk
1 cup liquid hot coffee

1. In a medium bowl, mix oil, sugar, and eggs.

2. In a separate bowl, sift together flour, dry baking cocoa, baking powder, and baking soda.

3. Add flour mixture alternately with buttermilk to sugar mixture. Beat well after each addition.

4. Stir in hot coffee. Batter will be lumpy.

5. Pour cake batter into a well-greased 9"×13" cake pan, or 2 round cake pans.

6. Bake at 350°F for 20–30 minutes, or until a toothpick inserted in center of cake comes out clean.

7. When cake is cool, frost with your favorite frosting.

Chocolate Cupcakes

Makes: 1 dozen cupcakes
Prep Time: 20 minutes
Baking Time: 10–15 minutes

1 cup sugar
1 egg
½ cup vegetable oil
1 cup dry baking cocoa
1 ½ cups flour
½ cup buttermilk
1 teaspoon baking soda
1 teaspoon vanilla extract
½ cup hot water

1. Combine sugar, egg, and oil in a large bowl. Mix well.

2. Add remaining ingredients, following the order listed. Beat well.

3. Line muffin pans with cupcake liners. Fill each liner ½ to ⅔ full.

4. Bake at 350°F for 10–15 minutes, or until a toothpick inserted into the center of a cupcake comes out clean.

5. Remove from the pans and allow to cool before frosting.

TIP:
Any cake recipe can be converted to cupcakes. Just bake in muffin tins instead of cake pans and bake for 10-15 minutes.

Christmas Cake

Makes: 1 two-layer cake
Prep Time: 20 minutes
Baking Time: 30–35 minutes
Cooling Time: 1 hour

¾ cup (1 ½ sticks) butter, softened
2 cups granulated sugar
4 eggs, separated
3 cups flour
4 teaspoons baking powder
1 cup milk
¾ cup chopped walnuts or pecans, *divided*

1. Cream butter and sugar together until well blended.

2. Separate eggs. Add egg yolks to creamed mixture. Beat well. (Reserve egg whites in a separate bowl.)

3. Stir flour and baking powder together in bowl.

4. Add milk alternately with flour and baking powder to creamed mixture, stirring well after each addition.

5. Stir in ½ cup chopped nuts.

6. Beat egg whites until frothy. Fold into batter.

7. Pour batter into 2 lightly greased 9" round cake pans.

8. Bake at 350°F for 30–35 minutes, or until toothpick inserted in centers comes out clean.

9. Cool cakes to room temperature.

10. Frost with Caramel Frosting (see page 160).

11. Sprinkle top with reserved nuts.

Caramel Frosting

Makes: 3–4 cups frosting
Prep Time: 5 minutes
Cooking Time: 5–10 minutes
Cooling Time: 1–2 hour

1 ½ cups brown sugar
¾ cup (1 ½ sticks) butter, cut into chunks
⅓ cup milk
1 teaspoon vanilla extract
3–4 cups confectioners' sugar

1. In a medium saucepan, combine brown sugar and butter. Heat until boiling, stirring continually. Allow to boil for 1 minute, stirring the whole time.

2. Add milk. Bring to boiling point again, stirring constantly.

3. Allow to cool to room temperature.

4. Stir in vanilla.

5. Stir in confectioners' sugar until the icing is spreadable, but not runny.

6. Spread on Christmas Cake (page 159), Chocolate Cupcakes (page 157), or Grandpa Cookies (page 154).

Seven-Minute Frosting

For: 1 cake
Prep Time: 15 minutes
Cooking Time: 7 minutes

2 egg whites
1 ½ cups sugar
⅓ cup cold water
1 tablespoon light corn syrup
1 teaspoon vanilla extract
¼ teaspoon cream of tartar
⅛ teaspoon salt

1. Separate eggs into 2 bowls: 1 for the whites; 1 for the yolks. Place whites in a medium saucepan. (Save yolks for another use.)

2. Combine all other ingredients with egg whites in the saucepan.

3. Bring mixture to a boil and allow to cook for 7 minutes.

4. With a mixer or egg beater, beat until light and fluffy.

5. Spread on cake and serve.

Jelly Roll

Makes: 8–10 servings
Prep Time: 20–30 minutes
Baking Time: 6–8 minutes
Cooling Time: 1 hour

4 eggs at room temperature
¼ teaspoon salt
¾ teaspoon baking powder
¾ cup granulated sugar
¾ cup cake flour
1 teaspoon vanilla extract

1. Combine eggs, salt, and baking powder. Beat with mixer, gradually adding sugar. Mixture will be light in color and slightly thickened.

2. Add cake flour and vanilla.

3. Line a 10"×15" baking pan with waxed paper. Grease waxed paper and sprinkle a little flour on top.

4. Pour batter onto waxed paper in pan.

5. Bake at 400°F for 6–8 minutes, or until toothpick inserted in center comes out clean.

6. Sprinkle powdered sugar onto a tea towel or a long stretch of waxed paper.

7. When jelly roll is finished baking, flip onto sugared tea towel or waxed paper.

8. Starting at the narrow end of the jelly roll, gently roll the tea towel and jelly roll together into a log shape.

9. Allow to cool completely.

10. When cooled, unroll the jelly roll and spread with filling (see page 163).

11. Roll up the jelly roll with filling inside.

12. To serve, place on platter or tray with the beginning of the roll facing down. Cut into 1"–2"-thick slices.

Jelly Roll Filling

Makes: Enough filling for 1 jelly roll
Prep Time: 15 minutes
Cooking Time: Approximately 5 minutes
Cooling Time: 1 hour

4 tablespoons flour
¼ cup brown sugar
¼ teaspoon salt
⅔ cup hot water
4 tablespoons (½ stick) butter, cut into chunks
1½ teaspoons vanilla extract
Food coloring, optional

1. In a small saucepan, combine flour, sugar, and salt.

2. Add water, stirring constantly, and heat until the mixture becomes smooth and thickens.

3. Remove from the heat. Stir in butter and vanilla until butter melts.

4. If you wish, stir in food coloring.

5. Allow to cool before spreading on cooled jelly roll.

Creamy Jelly Roll Topping

Makes: enough topping for 1 jelly roll
Prep Time: 10 minutes

8-ounce package cream cheese, softened to room temperature
9-ounce package frozen whipped topping, thawed
2 cups confectioners' sugar

1. In a good-sized bowl, beat cream cheese until creamy.

2. Fold in whipped topping.

3. Gently stir in confectioners' sugar, mixing well.

4. Spread mixture on cooled jelly roll before slicing it.

NOTE:
This topping can also be used as frosting for cupcakes.

Vanilla Cornstarch Pudding

Makes: 15–20 servings
Prep Time: 10 minutes
Cooking Time: 15 minutes
Chilling Time: 3–4 hours, or overnight

2 quarts milk

1½ cups sugar

3 heaping tablespoons cornstarch

5 eggs

1 teaspoon vanilla extract

8-ounce or 16-ounce package frozen whipped topping, thawed

1. In a large saucepan, heat milk until just to the boiling point, but do not boil.

2. In a bowl, beat sugar, cornstarch, and eggs together until foamy.

3. Add one cup of hot milk into egg mixture, stirring constantly until well mixed.

4. Slowly pour all of egg mixture into hot milk.

5. Stirring constantly, cook over low heat until thickened.

6. Remove from the heat and stir in vanilla.

7. Cool for 3–4 hours, or overnight.

8. Stir desired amount of whipped topping into chilled pudding just before serving.

TIP:
You can cut the ingredients of this large recipe in half and still have good results.

Banana Pudding

Makes: 25–30 servings
Prep Time: 20 minutes

3 (3.4-ounce) packages instant vanilla pudding
5 cups milk
2 (8-ounce) boxes vanilla wafers, *divided*
12–15 ripe bananas, sliced, *divided*
16-ounce container frozen whipped topping, thawed

1. Make vanilla pudding by following directions on the box, using the 5 cups milk.

2. In a very large bowl, or in 2 large bowls, make a layer of half the wafers, then a layer of half the sliced bananas, and a layer of half the pudding.

3. Repeat layers.

4. Top with a layer of whipped topping.

5. Cover and refrigerate until ready to serve.

TIPS:
Substitute crushed graham crackers instead of vanilla wafers if you wish.

This is enough pudding for a big party. You can make ⅓ of this recipe and serve 8–10 people.

Date Pudding

Makes: 20 servings
Prep Time: 30–45 minutes
Baking Time: 30–35 minutes
Cooling Time: 2–3 hours

1 cup chopped dates
1 teaspoon baking soda
1 tablespoon butter, softened
1 cup water
2 eggs
1 cup flour
1 cup sugar
1 teaspoon vanilla extract
¾ cup nuts, chopped

Sauce:
2 cups water
1 cup brown sugar
8 tablespoons (1 stick) butter
½ cup flour
2–3 tablespoons water
16-ounce package frozen whipped topping, thawed

My Aunt Vern from Ohio introduced us to this rich, nutty dessert when we visited. This pudding, which is really a trifle, is a three-layered concoction of pure, calorie-laden bliss.

1. In a large bowl, combine dates, baking soda, and butter.

2. Bring water to a boil.

3. Cover date mixture with boiling water. Mix well and let cool.

4. When dates are cool, add eggs, flour, sugar, vanilla, and chopped nuts. Stir well.

5. Pour mixture into well-greased 9"×13" baking pan.

6. Bake at 325°F for 30–35 minutes, or until a toothpick inserted in center comes out clean.

7. Allow to cool. Then cut pudding into 1" squares.

8. To make sauce, pour 2 cups water, brown sugar, and butter into medium saucepan. Bring to a boil, stirring frequently.

9. In a small bowl, blend flour with 2–3 tablespoons of water until smooth.

10. Stir flour mixture into hot syrup. Stir constantly and bring again to a boil.

11. Remove from the heat and cool completely.

12. To serve, layer ⅓ pudding squares on bottom of large bowl. Add ⅓ of sauce and ⅓ of whipped topping.

13. Repeat two more times until bowl is filled with three layers.

14. Cover. Chill in the refrigerator until ready to serve.

Cream Sticks

Makes: about 2½ dozen sticks
Prep Time: 20–30 minutes
Rising Time: 1¼–2½ hours
Frying Time: a few minutes per batch

1 cup milk
2 tablespoons yeast
1 cup warm water (110–115°F)
½ cup vegetable shortening
⅔ cup sugar
2 eggs, beaten
1 teaspoon salt
6 cups flour, *divided*
Vegetable oil for deep-frying

1. Heat milk until almost boiling. Remove from the heat and allow to cool.

2. In a small bowl, dissolve yeast in warm water.

3. In a large bowl, combine shortening, sugar, eggs, and salt.

4. Add milk and yeast mixture to shortening mixture.

5. Slowly add flour, 2–3 cups at a time. Mix in until dough is soft.

6. Cover and let rise until dough has doubled in size, approximately 1–2 hours.

7. Sprinkle flour on work area. Roll out dough on work area until ¼"–½" thick.

8. Cut dough into rectangles 4"×1" in size. Place on baking sheets about 1" apart.

9. Cover and let rise until dough is almost double in size, approximately 15–30 minutes.

10. To fry, heat vegetable oil in a large saucepan to 375°F.

11. Carefully drop 3 or 4 cream sticks at a time into hot oil and fry until golden brown, turning once.

12. Remove from oil and cool.

Doughnuts

Makes: 25–40 doughnuts
Prep Time: 45 minutes
Rising Time: 2–3 hours
Frying Time: 5–10 minutes
Cooling Time: 20 minutes

¾ tablespoon yeast
½ cup warm water (110–115°F)
1 cup milk
¼ cup granulated sugar
1 egg
½ cup mashed potatoes
¼ cup vegetable oil
¼ teaspoon salt
4 cups flour
5–6 pounds solid vegetable shortening

Glaze:
4 cups confectioners' sugar
6 tablespoons heavy whipping cream
2 tablespoons cornstarch
1 teaspoon vanilla extract
Water to thin glaze

1. Dissolve yeast in warm water and set aside.

2. In a large saucepan, heat milk and sugar just until hot. Do not boil.

3. In a separate bowl, beat egg.

4. Stir beaten egg, mashed potatoes, and vegetable oil into milk.

5. Add yeast mixture to milk mixture and stir well.

6. Add salt and flour. Beat well until dough is sticky.

7. Cover dough with plastic wrap or a tea towel. Let rise until double in size, approximately 1–2 hours.

8. Sprinkle the counter or tabletop liberally with flour to prevent dough from sticking. Line cookie sheets with waxed paper and sprinkle with flour.

9. Roll out dough on the work space until it is approximately ¼" thick.

10. With a doughnut cutter, or any circle-shaped cutter, cut out doughnuts.

(Continued on next page)

11. Place doughnuts on prepared cookie sheets. Cover. Allow them to rise until doubled in size, approximately 1 hour.

12. Melt shortening over medium heat until it reaches a temperature of 350–375°F.

13. Fry 3 or 4 doughnuts at a time, just until golden brown on top. Flip and brown on second side, watching carefully and removing quickly.

14. Using a colander, drain the shortening off the doughnuts.

15. Cool completely before glazing.

16. To make the glaze, mix confectioners' sugar, heavy whipping cream, cornstarch, and vanilla in a medium bowl. Add water until the glaze is the desired consistency.

17. To glaze the doughnuts, dip the doughnuts into the glaze, flipping them over so that glaze covers both sides.

18. Using a dinner fork or fingers, remove the doughnut and allow excess glaze to drip off.

Filling for Cream Sticks

Makes: cream for 2½ dozen sticks
Prep Time: 15–20 minutes

3 teaspoons flour
I cup milk
I cup vegetable shortening
I cup sugar
I tablespoon vanilla extract
2½ cups confectioners' sugar

1. In a small saucepan, combine flour and milk until it forms a smooth paste.

2. Bring to a boil, stirring constantly.

3. Remove from the heat and cool.

4. In a medium electric mixer bowl, beat together shortening, sugar, and vanilla.

5. Add flour and milk mixture. Stir well.

6. Beat in confectioners' sugar.

7. Cut slits in the cooled cream sticks to fill with filling. Use a cookie press or cake decorating kit to fill cream sticks.

Topping for Cream Sticks

Makes: Enough topping for 2½ dozen sticks
Prep Time: 10 minutes
Cooling Time: 1 hour

4 tablespoons (½ stick) butter
1 cup brown sugar
⅓ cup milk
½ cup vegetable shortening
2 cups confectioners' sugar

1. In a medium saucepan, melt butter.

2. Add brown sugar and milk.

3. Stirring frequently, bring mixture to a boil.

4. Remove from the heat and cool.

5. When mixture is cool, stir in shortening.

6. When smooth, stir in confectioners' sugar. Beat until smooth.

7. Spread on top of filled cream sticks.

Beverages

Lemonade

Makes: 1 gallon
Prep Time: 10 minutes
Standing Time: 10 minutes

2 cups sugar
3 lemons, sliced very thin
1 gallon water

1. Using a potato masher, pound sugar into pulp of lemon slices. Let stand 10 minutes.

2. Fish out the lemon slices and squeeze them, extracting as much juice as possible. Discard rinds.

3. Add water to sugar-pulp and ice to taste.

Meadow Tea to Drink Right Away

Makes: 1 ½ gallons
Prep Time: 10 minutes
Steeping Time: 10–15 minutes

2 cups fresh herb leaves (peppermint, spearmint, or whatever is growing in your garden)
1 ½ gallons water
Sugar to taste

1. Rinse tea leaves in cold water.

2. Bring the 1½ gallons fresh water to a boil.

3. Submerge tea leaves in boiling water and turn off burner.

4. Allow to steep 10–15 minutes.

5. Remove all tea leaves. Squeeze, without burning your hands, to extract all juice.

6. Add sugar to taste while tea is hot. Stir to dissolve.

7. Chill tea immediately. Serve with ice.

Meadow Tea Concentrate to Freeze

Makes: 6 quarts concentrate
Prep Time: 5 minutes
Cooking Time: 5 minutes
Sleeping Time: 6–7 hours, or overnight

24 cups water
6–8 cups sugar
12 cups fresh tea leaves

1. In a large pot, boil water and sugar for 5 minutes.

2. Add tea leaves. Submerge in hot water. Allow to steep 6–7 hours or overnight.

3. Strain tea.

4. Pour into containers and freeze.

5. To make tea, combine 3 parts water with 1 part tea.

Quick Homemade Root Beer

Makes: 1 gallon
Prep Time: 10 minutes
Steeping Time: 4 hours
Chilling Time: 8 hours, or overnight

2 cups sugar
4 teaspoons root beer extract
¾ teaspoon yeast
1 gallon lukewarm water, *divided*

1. In a small bowl, mix sugar, root beer extract, and yeast.

2. Pour into a 1-gallon jug.

3. Add ½ gallon lukewarm water.

4. Shake or stir until sugar is dissolved.

5. Add remaining ½ gallon of lukewarm water.

6. Cap tightly and set in the sun for 4 hours.

7. Chill overnight.

8. Serve the next day.

TIP:

A yummy way to enjoy root beer: Put one or two scoops of vanilla ice cream in the bottom of a glass. Pour root beer over ice cream. Stir and enjoy.

French Chocolate

Makes: 16–18 servings
Prep Time: 20 minutes

¾ cup chocolate chips
½ cup light corn syrup
⅓ cup water
1 teaspoon vanilla extract
1 pint whipping cream
2 quarts milk

1. In a medium saucepan, combine chocolate chips, corn syrup, and water. Heat over low heat until chips melt, stirring frequently.

2. Add vanilla and allow to cool.

3. In a separate bowl, beat cream until thick.

4. Adding a small portion at a time, slowly beat in chocolate mixture.

5. Place in the refrigerator until ready to use.

6. Before serving, heat milk to almost boiling.

7. Fill a favorite mug half-full of creamy chocolate mixture.

8. Fill to the top with hot milk.

9. Stir and serve.

Mam's Hot Chocolate

Makes: 4 servings
Prep Time: 5 minutes
Cooking Time: 10 minutes

¼ cup water
1 tablespoon powdered baking cocoa
3 tablespoons sugar
4 cups milk

1. Pour water, baking cocoa, and sugar into a medium saucepan. Boil for 2 minutes.

2. In a separate saucepan, heat milk just to boiling point.

3. Add chocolate mixture to warm milk and stir.

Hot Chocolate Mix

Prep Time: 5 minutes

8-quart package powdered milk
16-ounce container Nestlé Nesquik
1 pint nondairy coffee creamer
1 pound (2 cups) confectioners' sugar
1 bag mini-marshmallows, optional

1. Mix all ingredients.

2. Store in an airtight container.

3. To make one cup of hot chocolate, add boiling water to ⅓ cup of mix.

Conversion Charts

Metric and Imperial Conversions

(These conversions are rounded for convenience)

Ingredient	Cups/Tablespoons/Teaspoons	Ounces	Grams/Milliliters
Butter	1 cup/ 16 tablespoons/ 2 sticks	8 ounces	230 grams
Cheese, shredded	1 cup	4 ounces	110 grams
Cream cheese	1 tablespoon	0.5 ounce	14.5 grams
Cornstarch	1 tablespoon	0.3 ounce	8 grams
Flour, all-purpose	1 cup/1 tablespoon	4.5 ounces/0.3 ounce	125 grams/8 grams
Flour, whole wheat	1 cup	4 ounces	120 grams
Fruit, dried	1 cup	4 ounces	120 grams
Fruits or veggies, chopped	1 cup	5 to 7 ounces	145 to 200 grams
Fruits or veggies, pureed	1 cup	8.5 ounces	245 grams
Honey, maple syrup, or corn syrup	1 tablespoon	0.75 ounce	20 grams
Liquids: cream, milk, water, or juice	1 cup	8 fluid ounces	240 milliliters
Oats	1 cup	5.5 ounces	150 grams
Salt	1 teaspoon	0.2 ounce	6 grams
Spices: cinnamon, cloves, ginger, or nutmeg (ground)	1 teaspoon	0.2 ounce	5 milliliters
Sugar, brown, firmly packed	1 cup	7 ounces	200 grams
Sugar, white	1 cup/1 tablespoon	7 ounces/0.5 ounce	200 grams/12.5 grams
Vanilla extract	1 teaspoon	0.2 ounce	4 grams

Oven Temperatures

Fahrenheit	Celsius	Gas Mark
225°	110°	¼
250°	120°	½
275°	140°	1
300°	150°	2
325°	160°	3
350°	180°	4
375°	190°	5
400°	200°	6
425°	220°	7
450°	230°	8

Index